HowExpert Guide to the San Fernando Valley

101 Tips to Learn about the History, Celebrities, Entertainment, Dining, and Places to Visit and Explore in San Fernando Valley, California

HowExpert with Susan Hartzler

For more tips related to this topic, visit
HowExpert.com/sanfernandovalley

Recommended Resources

- HowExpert.com – Quick 'How To' Guides on All Topics from A to Z by Everyday Experts.
- HowExpert.com/free – Free HowExpert Email Newsletter.
- HowExpert.com/books – HowExpert Books
- HowExpert.com/courses – HowExpert Courses
- HowExpert.com/clothing – HowExpert Clothing
- HowExpert.com/membership – HowExpert Membership Site
- HowExpert.com/affiliates – HowExpert Affiliate Program
- HowExpert.com/jobs – HowExpert Jobs
- HowExpert.com/writers – Write About Your #1 Passion/Knowledge/Expertise & Become a HowExpert Author.
- HowExpert.com/resources – Additional HowExpert Recommended Resources
- YouTube.com/HowExpert – Subscribe to HowExpert YouTube.
- Instagram.com/HowExpert – Follow HowExpert on Instagram.
- Facebook.com/HowExpert – Follow HowExpert on Facebook.
- TikTok.com/@HowExpert – Follow HowExpert on TikTok.

Publisher's Foreword

Dear HowExpert Reader,

HowExpert publishes quick 'how to' guides on all topics from A to Z by everyday experts.

At HowExpert, our mission is to discover, empower, and maximize everyday people's talents to ultimately make a positive impact in the world for all topics from A to Z...one everyday expert at a time!

All of our HowExpert guides are written by everyday people just like you and me, who have a passion, knowledge, and expertise for a specific topic.

We take great pride in selecting everyday experts who have a passion, real-life experience in a topic, and excellent writing skills to teach you about the topic you are also passionate about and eager to learn.

We hope you get a lot of value from our HowExpert guides, and it can make a positive impact on your life in some way. All of our readers, including you, help us continue living our mission of positively impacting the world for all spheres of influences from A to Z.

If you enjoyed one of our HowExpert guides, then please take a moment to send us your feedback from wherever you got this book.

Thank you, and we wish you all the best in all aspects of life.

Sincerely,

BJ Min
Founder & Publisher of HowExpert
HowExpert.com

PS...If you are also interested in becoming a HowExpert author, then please visit our website at HowExpert.com/writers. Thank you & again, all the best!

Table of Contents

Chapter 1: The History of The San Fernando Valley

The suburb of the San Fernando Valley has very important roots when it comes to California history

Tip #1 The History

The history of the San Fernando Valley began long before the San Fernando Mission was established in 1797. The roots of the Valley date back to 1769, when the Spanish conquest of Mexico discovered what was then referred to as Alta California. But life in the Valley started way before that with small Native American tribes. And for more than 7,000 years, the Fernandeño and Chumash people lived off the land.

The original Valley inhabitants—more than 310,000 of them—took care of themselves and each other by hunting and fishing. Indigenous artifacts discovered in the area of leaching basins are proof that the tribes also gathered nuts and seeds and pulverized them into an edible mush. It is believed that they spoke more than 100 languages at the time.

Then came the building of the San Fernando Mission. It brought many people to the Valley, namely three families who relocated there from other missions in the United States. At that time, Spain was sending Franciscan priests to the states in order to spread Christianity with the establishment of twenty-one missions, of which San Fernando is the seventeenth.

The construction of the mission itself required workers and created jobs and traffic, something that the Valley is still known for today.

The large quadrangle building itself includes the original simple adobe church, with the padre's quarters, called a Convento, that branches off with a stunning colonnade of 19 arches that border the building. You'll find more details about the San Fernando Mission below.

Meantime, the rich soil of the Valley made it the perfect place for farmers and ranchers to live and work. Back then, the Valley was dotted with bucolic farms and ranchos. And in the early days, when the Valley was still under Mexican rule before the Conquest of California, which lasted from 1846 into 1847, cattle and sheep grazed the rolling hills. Big citrus and walnut groves and fruit orchards also grew there. Imagine how good it smelled? The orange blossoms from remnants of these orchards add a sweet smell to the Valley today, especially in the springtime when they bloom.

Even after the fighting ended in the Mexican-American War, thanks to the signing of the Treaty of Cahuenga, the ranching and farming continued. That's when Californians were allowed to peaceable return to their property and begin working the land again.

The end of the Civil War meant a new beginning for the Valley, which was still an agricultural area. With all that farming and ranching, it's not surprising to note that the Valley was formed around reliable water supplies through a large-scale irrigation system. However, after the war ended, even with the new irrigation, a series of droughts convinced men with names like Lankershim and Van Nuys to begin dry farming of wheat and barley crops. Later, their names were used for major thoroughfares and communities of the Valley.

Then with the completion of the Southern Pacific rail line in 1874, the Valley drew even more settlers. The rail line gave more access to the land, and it's that proximity to transportation routes through the surrounding mountains made it an even more popular destination. So, it was water and transportation that put the Valley on the map.

It wasn't until 1915 when the Valley was annexed, that the area started to become what it is today—a place filled with the stories that movies are made from. These tales include the following:

- Norma Jeane Mortenson, better known as the glamorous actress and model Marilyn Monroe, was discovered while working at a defense plant in Van Nuys.
- Beverly Hills may be the home of the motion picture academy, but North Hollywood has the television academy, complete with an enormous golden Emmy statue out front. Selfie anyone?
- Even today, Pierce College offers visible proof of the Valley's agricultural past. One of the Valley's community colleges, located in Woodland Hills, still teaches agriculture and farming. Now more than 75 years old, locals used to head to Pierce to buy their milk and eggs courtesy of the cows and chickens in the ag program's working farm. The farm's still there, and it's still working today. So is the college's weather station, which is one of the oldest in the entire nation.
- When the Red Car rail lines arrived in 1912, the Valley still had no undertaker, so a designated death car carried the Valley's deceased over the pass and into LA for the undertaking.
- More recently, since the 1980s, the Valley has had its own called Valleyspeak or Valspeak associated with Valley girls. That's when the song *Valley Girl* hit the charts. Written by Frank Zappa and performed by the artist and his daughter Moon Zappa, the song highlighted the distinctive speech patterns of the valley youth culture of the time. That culture was already receiving recognition in the media, but the song made it famous. Well, the song is in the 1983 film *Valley Girl*. These two things converging at the same time were

based on the socio-economic stereotype of the Valley girl. Think ditzy white-blonde girl hanging out in the local mall because "OMG, it's like, totally bitchin," a stereotype drowning in materialism and air headedness. As the public consciousness became inundated with the distinct Valley girl accent, the true demographics of the area became buried and under-represented. Good or bad, that stereotype and its language "like" stuck. Even today, the stereotypical Valley girl speak is prevalent among most teenage girls influenced by pop culture not only in the Valley but all over the USA.

- Other Valley-focused films like *Heathers* and *Clueless* perpetuated and parodied the Valley girl stereotype. But today, scholars who have studied the dialect and lifestyle claim the rising inflection does not only represent a shallow Valley girl but holds a range of meanings, especially when it comes to different geographical areas. In any case, today, Valley girl speak is still popular and used by both men and women.

Today, the Valley is well known as home to iconic film studios like Warner Bros. Studio and Walt Disney Studios. In addition, it is home to the Universal Studios Hollywood theme park.

Tip #2 The Basics

Today, the San Fernando Valley is more than just strip malls, mini-marts, freeway overpasses, and suburban sprawl. The 250-ish square miles create a dynamic place in its own right where more than 1.7 million live today. That makes the Valley one of the largest suburban areas in all of California, possibly the nation. Surrounded by the San Gabriel, Santa Susana, and Santa Monica mountains, as well as the hills of the Simi Valley, make for spectacular views, especially in the winter when you can see snow on the mountains.

The residents here are diverse, with Spanish, Korean, Thai, Armenian, Hebrew, Persian, Russian, Tagalog, Vietnamese, and

Hindi. Because of this diversity, many other languages are spoken here besides English.

The Valley's natural habitat is temperate, with grasslands, shrublands, and chaparral shrub forest as the norm. Residents enjoy a subtropical Mediterranean climate that's more hot than not. In fact, the summers here are long, hot, and dry, and the winters are short (and still hot, by the way) with chilly nights and intermittent rainfall. Plants species such as chamise, California lilac, and scrub oak dominate the Valley's ecosystem with remands of fruit trees from the old days.

Tip #3 Cities of the Valley

The Valley contains six incorporated cities:

- **Burbank**

Because it's the home of Disney and Warner Brothers, Burbank is known in the entertainment industry as the Media Capital of the World. However, it didn't start that way. The name Burbank came from an early resident—San Francisco dentist David Burbank who bought 9,200 acres of farmland there in 1866. After moving here, Burbank built himself a ranch house and spent the next 20 years herding sheep. Dr. Burbank is remembered today through a 12-foot statue of him installed in 2010 at the corner of Victory and Burbank Blvd. The statue itself was carved in Italy for more than half-a-million dollars.

In the 1940s, Burbank emerged as the center of both the entertainment and the aircraft industries. It quickly became known as an archetypal suburb of the 1950s and 60s—the perfect place to raise a family. Many popular TV shows were (and still are) filmed in

Burbank. Two of the most famous are *Laugh-In* and *The Tonight Show,* both of which ridiculed their sleepy hometown.

But even back then, the Valley was no joke. In fact, WWII planes were made at Lockheed Corp, where more than 90,000 worked during the mid-1970s. At that time, Lockheed brought in more money than any other Valley business.

Besides, it's home to the headquarters of the happiest place on earth since the Disney empire moved to Buena Vista Street in 1940. And then there's the fact that the original Starship Enterprise was built in Burbank. What more could a city brag about?

- **Calabasas**

In the foothills of the Santa Monica Mountains, you'll find a small haven called Calabasas. Native Americans, Spanish explorers, squatters, and bandits are all part of Calabasas' history. Way back when the Chumash Indians led a peaceful life amidst the rolling hills. These indigenous people made their homes in the Calabasas surrounded by streams and springs that offered a healthy supply of wildlife to sustain them. As a result, it was the Chumash Indians who named the area Calabasas. Researchers believe that word descended from the Indian word for "where geese fly," a fitting portrayal of this intimate, luxury community where residents can own horses and livestock (as pets), even today. Still, another school of thought says the name comes from the Spanish word for pumpkin. Well, that works too, especially around Halloween when you'll find lots of pumpkin patches open to the public.

One of the striking things you'll notice when you enter Calabasas is the stately and mature oak trees. As you read above, the native people counted on nuts like acorns from these trees to stay alive.

And the trees you see there today could be the same ones those American Indians saw because some of the oaks in Calabasas are believed to be more than 700-years-old.

After the turn of the century, several select spots in Calabasas became popular places to vacation at the turn of the century. So, developers began to create a serene place for weekend respites from the city. The Stunt family developed a homestead there on the north slope of Saddle Peak. This is still a favorite spot for filming motion pictures today, including such films as *Tarzan, The Adventures of Robin Hood,* and *Stalag 17*. In addition, an adobe home built in Calabasas in 1863 near the park by a settler named Sepulveda for his wife and twelve children is now in the process of being restored. It is believed to be the oldest home in the Los Angeles area.

Today, Calabasas is a celebrity hideaway. Stars from Kim Kardashian, Khloe Kardashian, Kourtney Kardashian, Kris Jenner, Kanye West, Drake, French Montana, Iggy Azalea, Justin Bieber, Miley Cyrus, The Weeknd, Will Smith, and Jessica Simpson all live or have lived there. And *Keeping Up with the Kardashians* was filmed there, which, besides making the Kardashian tribe famous, the show played a pivotal role in putting this hidden gem of a city on the map.

- **Glendale**

Located at the very southeastern corner of the valley, Glendale has its own Hollywood connection. The quaint town is home to several Hollywood production facilities and one super famous celebrity cemetery.

Originally inhabited by the Tongva people—also known as People of the Earth—Jose Maria Verdugo was given Rancho San Rafael in

1798 from then from Governor Diego de Borica. Verdugo, who was a corporal in the Spanish Army, was already farming the land when he took possession and left his mark on the area. Well, actually, it was his grandson Teodoro Verdugo who left his mark when he built the Catalina Verdugo Adobe, the oldest building in Glendale. The property also has the Oak of Peace growing on it—the sacred site making the end of the Mexican American War.

It wasn't until 1884 that residents gathered with the intent of forming a town site. They chose the name "Glendale," Gallic for valley of fertile, low-lying land.

One of the main attractions here is The Forest Lawn Cemetery, which opened in 1906. Even today, this cemetery where the Hollywood elite rest in peace is a place that must be seen to be believed. The park's sheer size is overwhelming, featuring rolling green hills on more than 300 acres dotted with white sculptures and old-world English chapels.

More than a million people visit Forest Lawn each year. Interesting fact: more than 60,000 people were married there—including Ronald Reagan, who tied the knot with Jane Wyman at the "Wee Kirk' o the Heather" chapel back in 1940.

Getting married at a cemetery might sound weird, but Forest Lawn isn't your ordinary run-of-the-mill cemetery. Instead, it's the resting place of the stars from Clark Gable and Nat King Cole to Walt Disney and Jean Harlow. Plus, it's the home of a world-class museum with an impressive art collection of marble and bronze sculptures, historic stained-glass windows, and masterpieces from the Gothic and Renaissance eras.

- **Hidden Hills**

There are no sidewalks or streetlights in the gated community of Hidden Hills. Instead, you'll find plenty of *"Horses and children at play"* signs. These signs are part of the charm here, along with the abundant 2-acre lots with exclusive, luxury homes built through strict standards that the leaders of this unique community uphold.

Residents say Hidden Hills exudes a certain rough-around-the-edges appeal—bringing a tranquil, bucolic scene from the past back to life in the present. The exclusive town is located right next to Calabasas and is known for being extremely quaint and low-key. Only about 506 families live here, making the total number of residents fewer than 2000.

The entire city is literally gated. Hence the name. In fact, approximately 95% of Hidden Hills is situated behind a gate. This is just one of many reasons celebrities have chosen to buy up real estate there. Past and present celebrity residents include rapper Drake, musician Miley Cyrus, Rapper French Montana, who purchased actress/singer Selena Gomez's Hidden Hills compound, Lee Ann Rimes, and Eddie Cibrian, Jessica Simpson, Ozzy and Sharon Osbourne, The Weeknd. Even superstar Angelina Jolie rented Denise Richard's Hidden Hills Estate at one time.

But it wasn't always the place of glitz and glamour. In fact, the super-private enclave started back in the early 1950s when two oak trees on a long dirt road alongside rolling hills were all that was there. That's when A.E. Hanson began his development of Hidden Hills.

It all began in 1950 with a large sign on Ventura Boulevard that said: *"1,000 Acres of Elbow Room - Live in Hidden Hills Where Living is Fun."* In an effort to get people to relocate there, Hanson built two model homes there. Interesting fact: Hanson also developed the exclusive community of Rolling Hills on the Palos Verdes Peninsula. He knew a thing or two about creating luxury, and his model homes showed how wonderful life could be there. While building the community, Hansen created the framework of governance that still serves the community today, the main element being an Architectural Committee that has been in existence for more than 50 years.

Then in 1957, a man named Lamond Chamberlain became the second major developer of Hidden Hills, taking over Hanson's remaining undeveloped land and becoming the first President of Hidden Hills Estates Inc.

Hidden Hills is the birthplace of the "Church on Horseback" concept. Back in the day (and even now), the area was known for being horse country. Then, in the summer of 1959, a six-year-old resident remarked, "Wouldn't it be fun if we could sit on our ponies and horses for church?" That's when "Church on Horseback" officially started. An outdoor devotional worship service for people of all ages, especially those who loved the great outdoors and horses. Why yes, please. Families attended the services not only on ponies and horses but also on donkeys, in buggies, and in surreys. Imagine the selfies you could have taken back then!

- **San Fernando**

This suburban city located near the foothills of the San Gabriel Mountains in the Valley's northern section has an impressive Latin American cultural charisma. This place holds the distinction of being the oldest city in the Valley, founded in 1874. It has earned its nickname of "The Mission City" since it is where the San Fernando Mission is located. Residents say it eludes spirituality.

Today, residents enjoy a high quality of life, where safety and community values are extremely important. But it wasn't always that way. In fact, following the mission's secularization in 1834, the area went into decline and was abandoned about a decade later.

San Fernando was originally populated by the Gabrielino and Tataviam Indians tribes before Spanish explorers passed through the region in 1769. In the nineteenth century, the hills and valleys of San Fernando were shaded by oak and walnut trees with a rugged landscape perfect for ranches and farms, and the area was home to a mixture of Spanish, Indian, and Mexican residents.

The city was founded in 1874 during a land boom in Southern California, compliments of the Southern Pacific Railroad's new rail line between Bakersfield and Los Angeles through Fremont Pass. As a result, an influx of people settled here, making San Fernando the railroad's "gateway to the north." Architecture was the main form of employment thanks to the Mediterranean climate combined with natural irrigation water from deep wells. In no time, the community became known for cultivating citrus and olives along with an abundance of other vegetables and fruits.

That independent water supply was of utmost importance since it allowed San Fernando to remain autonomous and incorporated in 1911. Most of the Valley's other communities became part of Los Angeles in 1915 to take advantage of the Los Angeles Aqueduct, which started flowing in 1913. See? We told you water was a big part of the Valley's history.

Today, the population of about 22,600 people makes San Fernando one of the valley's smaller communities. But, with its Mexican heritage reflected in the downtown architecture, the city has retained its own individuality. As far as its unique identity, the annual Fiesta celebration of its Mission days takes place each year. It is also the site of the annual Indigenous Peoples Day Celebration with an array of diverse performances, including an authentic Pow Wow, Aztec music and dance, food, drum circles, and more.

- **Los Angeles**

The Los Angeles area of the Valley is made of several neighborhoods, including Northridge, Arleta, Canoga Park, Chatsworth, Encino, Granada Hills, Lake View Terrace, Mission Hills, North Hollywood, North Hills, Pacoima, Panorama City, Porter Ranch, Reseda, Sherman Oaks, Studio City, Sun Valley, Sunland, Sylmar, Tarzana, Toluca Lake, Tujunga, Van Nuys, Valley Village, West Hills, Winnetka, and Woodland Hills.

We're talking about the ultimate in suburban lifestyle combining urban living with access to the natural beauty. In addition, the surrounding countryside lends an air of Mother Nature that you won't find in other areas of the golden state.

Again, the region was originally settled by the native Gabrielino or Tongva people. They built and lived in dome-shaped houses until the Spanish explorers came to the region in the 1700s. All of it was referred to as Zelzah, the same name as a major thoroughfare in the Valley and the original name of Northridge. This area was home to fresh water fed by underground streams that still run beneath the area. Water, again.

Today, the area receives an A or A+ grade in housing, weather, and amenities and has a total Livability score of 80. All that makes the Los Angeles portion of the Valley 8% above the national average as far as quality of life goes.

The Valley's 260 square miles are found in a centralized location that provides easy access to everything Los Angeles has to offer—because of this, staying in the Valley is your best choice when visiting. Plus, it's in the suburbs, so it's very family-friendly and not as expensive as its neighbors. Some of the places to check out include:

- **Hollywood**

When you think of the entertainment business, Hollywood always comes to mind. And for good reason. Hollywood is the home to such famous landmarks as Grauman's Chinese Theatre, a movie palace on the historic Hollywood Walk of Fame, Paramount Classic Hollywood studio, with its historic and still active backlot tours, historic music venues such as the Hollywood Bowl, an amphitheater in the Hollywood Hills, and the Dolby Theatre (formerly the Kodak Theater), home of the Academy Awards Ceremony. You can also get to some great hiking spots like Runyan Canyon, which overlooks the Hollywood Sign. And who could forget horseback riding to the Hollywood sign?

Malibu can be reached by the 101 north through Las Virgenes. Signs direct drivers to the coast; however, if you see local surfers pass you on the Las Virgenes Canyon, a passenger in a passing car with a surfboard on top gives you a thumbs-up sign, which means the waves are good. Don't miss visiting Zuma Beach or the Malibu Lagoon State Beach. And keep an eye out for celebrities since Malibu is a favorite among the rich and famous. Stars like Jennifer Aniston, Brad Pitt, Cindy Crawford, Courteney Cox, Steven Spielberg, Patrick Dempsey, Paris Hilton, Charlie Sheen, and Ellen DeGeneres have all lived there at one time or another. However, you'll never know the exact place since the residents of the tony Malibu Colony, famous for its famous residents, are kept secret, and the beaches there are private. But you might see someone famous at a local restaurant, shop, or even getting gas on Pacific Coast Highway.

- **Six Flags Magic Mountain**

Just north of the Valley adjacent to the I-5 Freeway, you'll find a 262-acre theme park. An alternative to driving is to take the Metrolink to the Santa Clarita Train Station. From there, you can easily hop on a connecting bus to the amusement park. And no parking hassles!

- **Santa Monica**

The famous beach town of Santa Monica is accessible by heading south on the 405 freeway. Here's an important tip: don't try to take the 405 during rush hour traffic! You'll be stalled for hours! But the drive is nice, and you'll see The Getty Center Museum as you head over the hill. The actual beach is next to Palisades Park, where the views over the Pacific Ocean are stunning and where you'll find the homes of J.J. Abrams, Ben Affleck, and Judd Apatow.

You should also be sure to walk on the Santa Monica Pier, where you'll find the Pacific Park amusement park with its Hippodrome Carousel, a Ferris wheel that looks out over the ocean. Also located in Santa Monica, Bergamot Station is the home of several art galleries. Check the website for events there.

- **Simi Valley**

Near the 118 Freeway, you'll find the Reagan Presidential Library and Air Force One Pavilion. Simi is surrounded by the Santa Susana Mountains, which had a nuclear reactor housed there, and it is believed that there is still nuclear material in the soil. Simi is also known as the location of the Rodney King trial.

- **The Westside**

Home to the Getty Center, the iconic Playboy Mansion, and UCLA, the Westside can be reached by taking the 405 Freeway south. You can also get to the Getty via Metro Rapid 761, with a bus that stops right in front. But the Getty isn't the only museum or cultural destination found on the Westside. The largest art museum in the western United States, the Los Angeles County Museum of Art (LACMA), is located there. Neighborhoods like Beverly Hills, Brentwood, Bel-Air, West Hollywood, Century City, and Culver City are practically as famous as the residents who call the Westside home, such as Channing Tatum, as well as Beyonce, and Jay Z.

Tip #4 The Valley's Celebrity Connection

As you read above, the hillside communities in the Valley, many of the exclusive, luxury homes of the Valley, offer stunning views of the ocean, downtown Los Angeles, and at night, the sparkling lights of the Valley floor are amazing. And while the homes on the Valley side of the Santa Monica Mountains may not include those breathtaking views, many residents still get to enjoy sweeping vistas of the San Gabriel Mountains.

Homes in the Valley rest on large lots. The feeling of spaciousness in the Valley is only enhanced by the fact that these lots are built far apart from one another. A portion of Northridge is so sprawling that it is referred to today as Sherwood Forest.

The Valley is attractive to many in the entertainment industry because the location itself is somewhat removed from the spotlight of Hollywood. By living in the Valley, A-listers can feel somewhat removed from the buzz of Hollywood. And then there's the added value of some major studios being located right there and easy access to the ones that are found on the other side of the hill. For these reasons, stars and many people who work behind the scenes in Hollywood still choose the Valley for their home base. And as stated above, it is the perfect vacation base.

The Valley's famous celebrity residents date back to the early days of the silver screen and include superstars of today. Here's a partial list:

Referred to as the First Couple of Chatsworth, Roy Rogers and Dale Evans famously called the Valley home. Even Roy's famous golden palomino stallion, Trigger, spent time in the Valley when he retired in 1957, living out his final years in a stable near Roy's Chatsworth home. The Hollywood Power Couple's big ranch estate later became the place where Val Kilmer grew up. You might remember Kilmer as Batman, one of the many roles he played over the years. His current Netflix show, Val, includes footage from his Chatsworth home. It's very interesting to watch where this superstar grew up and how the Valley influenced his work and life.

Back then, Chatsworth was a popular place to live for many of the rich and famous, including many celebrities. Even Lucy loved the Valley. Yes, Lucille Ball and her husband Desi Arnaz were in their 20s when they purchased Desilu Ranch in Chatsworth. They shared their home with lots of animals, including hundreds of baby chickens and a cow who reportedly stuck his head through the couple's bedroom window for a kiss good night.

Barbara Stanwyck owned a large French and English Tudor-inspired eleven-acre ranch in Northridge. Northridge only had 40 residents at that time, and there was no grocery store or other necessities in the area. But the sparse land attracted Stanwyck, who loved horses and horse racing. The area attracted Zeppo Marx too for the same reasons. The brother of Groucho, Harpo, and Chico bought an adjoining 87-acres, and the two combined their properties to create a thoroughbred ranch together. The 100-acre ranch named Marwyck was the breeding ground for horses that ran and won on tracks across America. Actor William Holden and his wife, actress Janet Gaynor became neighbors of Marx and Stanwyck, buying yet another ranch in Northridge. Now that's a lot of star power in a small town like Northridge. It's also an important part of the history of the Valley.

Mae West spent a lot of time moving around the Valley. At first, she resided in a property on Rayen Street in North Hills called the Mae West Ranch. She also owned ten acres in Valleywood that she bought in 1935 for her father and sister to live with their trotter horses. Later, in 1938, the famous actress of stage and film purchased fifty acres in El Tono Estates, which was either located in today's Tarzana, Canoga Park, West Hills, or Woodland Hills, depending on who you ask.

When you think of the stars of *Gone with The Wind*, Clark Gable, and Carole Lombard, most likely, you don't think of the Valley. But you should. They lived in Encino on a 20-acre property called Shadow Ranch. Besides the quaint home, the property had its own cow barn, horse stables, and pigsty where no pigs lived, by the way, which they purchased for $50,000 from the director and actor Raoul Walsh. You may have never heard of Walsh, but he is considered a Hollywood legend himself with his 52-year directorial career.

Bob Hope lived in Toluca Lake, where he had many real estate holdings. It all started when he built a compound for his wife, Dolores, and their four children inside a walnut grove back in 1939. His 15,000 square-foot house that rested on 5.16-acres had an indoor pool. The Hopes had many famous visitors over the years, including Richard Nixon, whose helicopter actually landed directly on the backyard lawn so that the two men could play a round of golf at Lakeside Golf Club, located near Bob's home. Other famous visitors included Lucille Ball and Jack Benny. At one point, Hope owned more than 10,000 acres in the Valley.

Bing Crosby and his family lived in an extravagant Toluca Lake home, too, but their time in the Valley ended in tragedy. They lived in the home from the time it was first built in 1936 until it practically burnt down to the ground from a Christmas tree fire, of all things, in 1943. The fire caused more than $200,000 in damage and included Crosby's pipe collection, his many personal golf trophies, and his many recordings--a complete collection, by the way. The family also lost their beloved cocker spaniel in the blaze, but, luckily, Crosby's family escaped injury. The charred remains were sold then the home was fully restored to become home sweet home to other celebrities, including Micky Dolenz of the Monkees, one of the most successful bands of the 1960s, Andy Griffith, best known as the Sheriff in The Andy Griffith sitcom, and Jerry Van Dyke, the younger brother of Dick Van Dyke who was an actor, comedian, and musician in his own right.

Frank Sinatra's Farralone House, located in Chatsworth, would have a lot to say if walls could talk. Built in the 1950s during Old Blue Eye's Rat Pack days, major Hollywood celebrities hung out at the mid-century residence over the years. Originally built for a banking heiress by William Pereira, an architect famous for his futuristic designs, the sleek, single-story home itself is a star of the silver screen, appearing in *Bewitched, Big Little Lies, Mad Men, Californication, Transformers*, and more. Many Valley homes are used in movies and on television shows or commercials. Many Valley homeowners hire agents for their properties.

Entertainers Jane Meadows and Steve Allen lived in a 7,500+ square-foot ranch-style mansion on a hilltop in Encino. The mid-century estate sat on more than a full acre of land. Built in 1951, the couple took special care of their home over the years, ultimately living there for a total of 57 years! That's quite a commitment in the entertainment industry.

Former quarterback John Elway spent his high school years living in the Valley. He and his twin sister Jana attended Granada Hills High School. The school named its football field after the two-time Super Bowl winner, while the NFL presented the school with a gold football to honor the Denver Bronco.

Valerie Bertinelli, best known for her role as Barbara Cooper in *One Day at a Time*, grew up in the Valley and attended Granada Hills High School at the same time as Elway. The winner of two Golden Globe awards spent much of her childhood moving due to her father's job in the automotive industry. When the family landed in the Valley, Valerie met the producer father of one of her friends, and the rest is Hollywood history.

The almost seven-foot-tall actor Ted Cassidy, aka Lurch from *The Addams Family*, spent his final days living in the Valley at a ranch-style home in Woodland Hills. His cremated remains are buried in an unmarked location on the grounds. It sounds like a good movie plot, right?

Actor Jack Klugman, best remembered for his role as Oscar Madison in *The Odd Couple,* lived for a time in Woodland Hills too. Technically, he didn't own the estate. It was the property of his girlfriend at the time, who later became his second wife, Peggy Crosby. And if her last name sounds familiar, that's because Peggy was the ex-wife of Bing Crosby's son, Phillip. Blood runs deep in the Valley.

Actor and director Buster Keaton lived on a one-and-a-half-acre estate in Woodland Hills. He bought the property, which he referred to as a ranch, in 1947 with the money he earned from selling his life story to Paramount Pictures. Before that, the couple lived for years with Buster's family. Being the only movie star in town gave the silent film star certain advantages, like being referred to as the Mayor of Woodland Hills. They were a constant in Valley society until Buster's death in 1966.

In the 1930s, Harry Warner of Warner Brothers Studio fame owned a thousand-acre working ranch in Woodland Hills to raise thoroughbred horses. Part of his land is Warner Center, where today you can find homes and businesses but no racehorses. Not to be confused with Burbank's Warner Ranch, aka Columbia Ranch, the location for many movies and TV shows, including *Friends,* where the ranch was featured each week in the opening credits. Today, you can take a studio tour located only about a mile from the main studio lot.

Academy Award Winning Western star Arthur Hunnicutt lived in Northridge and was that community's honorary Mayor. The ranch-style home had a huge front yard where Arthur would greet the neighborhood children walking to and from school.

Robert Redford's 1990 diss in the LA Times still stings for present Valley residents. He is reported to have said: "When we moved to the Valley, I felt like I was being tossed into quicksand. There was no culture." Still, he did his time in the quicksand.

A-listers George Clooney, Samuel Jackson, Will Smith, Cynthia Basinet, Horace Bell, Lisa Bonet, John S. Boskovich, the entire Kardashian tribe, Selma Gomez, Nicole Eggert, and Kim Basinger all have or had Valley digs.

In her younger years, Susan Sontag self-edited the school newspaper in her North Hollywood high school. Later, she used those writing skills for books examining modern culture in both books and articles.

Before North Hollywood High opened, there were just two high schools in the Valley, Birmingham High School in Van Nuys and Canoga Park High School in Canoga Park. The famous celebrities who attended Birmingham include Marilyn Monroe and Sally Field. Meantime, Bryan Cranston attended Canoga Park High School. All those celebs lived somewhere in the Valley.

Ray Romano, best known as the star of *Everybody Loves Raymond*, lived in a gated community in Woodland Hills. He won three Emmys for the role of sportswriter and family man, Raymond, Ray, and Barone.

Richard Pryor lived in Northridge. While living there on June 9, 1980, the legendary comedian shocked the world when he accidentally spilled 151 proof rum on his shirt, setting himself ablaze with a cigarette lighter. He was free-basing cocaine at the time.

Matt LeBlanc and Kaley Cuoco live in Tarzana, not together, by the way. Don't want to start any rumors here. But we can tell you that both have been seen at the local Whole Foods stocking up on groceries.

Bravo star of the *Real Housewives of Beverly Hills*, Denise Richards, owned a Hidden Hills resort-like mansion that had a dog hotel on the property. After the season she starred in wrapped, she wanted to get out of town and was headed for Montana. Her Valley home was sold by Josh Altman of Bravo's *Million Dollar Los Angeles* fame, who also represented Kim Kardashian and Kanye West when they sold their property. See? It's all in the family!

Entertainer Wayne Brady apparently liked living in the Valley. He liked it so much that over the years, he lived in Woodland Hills for a time, then Tarzana and, most recently, Sherman Oaks in a gated modern home complete with spectacular views of the Valley's majestic Mountains.

The world-famous Jackson family lived in a two-acre compound in Encino. With its Cape Cod-style main house, guest house, swimming pool, tennis court, and more, the compound called Hayvenhurst was purchased back in 1971 with the money made by the initial Jackson 5 success.

- **Celebrity Spotting in the Valley**

Celebrity fascination is everything these days. Makes sense with the popularity of social media. And anyway, humans are social creatures, programmed to pay attention to the people at the top. The good news is the Valley is filled with famous people. And anyone who travels here might, just might, bump into one doing their everyday things. So if you want to see your favorite superstar, here are the best places to hang out in the Valley include:

Near Calabasas:

- Marmalade Café
- Lovi's Delicatessen
- The Six Chow House
- Pedalers Fork
- The Calabasas Commons
- Malibu Creek State Park
- Saddle Peak Lodge
- The Malibu Hindu Temple
- King Gillette Ranch

Near Westlake Village:

- Club 14 Wine Bar
- Smart & Final
- The Oaks Shopping Mall
- The Lakes Shopping Center
- Mastro's Steakhouse
- Yamato
- Point Magu State Park

Near Woodland Hills:

- Health Nut
- Leo & Lily
- The Local Peasant
- Bobby's Coffee Shop
- JOEY
- Inn of the Seventh Ray
- Westfield Topanga & The Village

Near Sherman Oaks:

- Blu Jam Café
- Anejo Cantina and Grill
- Casa Vega
- The Sherman
- GRANVILLE
- Firefly
- On The Thirty
- Oasis Bar & Restaurant
- Gelson's
- Sweet Butter
- Runyan Canyon
- Westfield Fashion Square
- Sherman Oaks Galleria

Near Tarzana:

- Whole Foods
- Aroma Coffee and Tea Co
- IHOP
- Waffle Love

Near Studio City:

- Erewhon Market
- The Studio City Farmer's Market
- The Rendition Room
- The Front Yard
- Granville
- Laurel Tavern
- The Tower Bar
- Black Market Liquor Bar

Tip #5 The Valley's Music Scene

You probably never heard about the popular 1940s movie starring a singing cowboy called *San Fernando Valley,* but did you know that

Bing Crosby, the country's most popular singer at the time, made the theme into a hit song? In fact, the Crosby song shot to No. 1 on the pop charts. But, of course, that was long before the dawn of the rock 'n' roll era when the San Fernando Valley began producing not only number one hit songs but also plenty of prominent musicians.

It all started in the late 1950s when teenage Chicano rocker Ritchie Valens helped put Pacoima on the map with his songs "Donna" and "La Bamba." His follow-up single, "Come On, Let's Go," was hugely popular too. Valens may have had a brief career, but he influenced many musicians over the years, from Carlos Santana, Los Lonely Boys, and Los Lobos to Stray Cats, The Blasters, and more.

From the mid-1960s to the early 1970s, all sorts of creative people from all over the country congregated in the Valley. It had to do with one of the hot buttons at the time, the Vietnam War. Many of those opposed to the war headed to Laurel Canyon, a winding road connecting the Valley with Hollywood, where music icons like Linda Ronstadt, Joni Mitchell, Neil Young, James Taylor, Carole King, Jackson Browne, the Mamas and the Papas, The Byrds, Eagles, Frank Zappa, and David Crosby lived, all protesters of the war. With big names in folk, rock, and pop like those, it's not hard to see how the area became quite the music scene.

The Valley became so central to the music scene that two months before Woodstock, more than 200,000 people landed at Devonshire Downs for *Newport '69*. The open-air concert took place over an entire weekend with a memorable performance from Creedence Clearwater Revival, Marvin Gaye, Jethro Tull, and Jimi Hendrix.

By the early 1980s, the Valley became a haven for the punk rock movement. Three members of the first punk band in the area, *Bad*

Religion, attended El Camino Real Charter High School in Woodland Hills. The '82 debut LP *How Could Hell Be Any Worse* came out on their own indie label, Epitaph Records.

It was *Bad Religion's* music videos that made the band popular—so popular that they were featured on the MTV show *120 Minutes*. By the 1990s, when punk went mainstream, *Bad Religion* became even more popular, benefitting from commercial alt-rock music. The band's success continued with regular album releases on a regular basis for years until 2013's *True North*.

Several Valley bands kept the spotlight on the Valley following the success of *Bad Religion*. *Linkin Park,* for example, burst onto the scene in 1996. Three band members of the nu-metal group were Agoura Hills High School alumni. All the musicians that made up the band *Hoobastank* also hailed from Agoura Calabasas, while members from the quintet *Incubus* grew up in Calabasas.

The three sisters who made up the group *HAIM* grew up in Valley Village. The girls performed with their parents at events, fairs, and festivals. Meantime, two of the sisters joined the classic rock cover band *Rockinhaim*, which was signed to Columbia Records. One of their songs was included in the soundtrack for the film, *The Sisterhood of the Travelling Pants*.

Here are some other musicians with ties to the Valley:

- Cherrie Currie from *The Runaways*, Dave Grohl from *Foo Fighters* and *Nirvana*, Tom Petty, Motown songwriter Lamont Dozier, Al Jarreau, and the Jackson family have ties to Encino.
- *Berlin's* Terri Nunn hosted a weekly radio show on KCSN-FM at Cal State Northridge.

- In gospel music, Grammy and Dove-winning Andrae Crouch became the Senior Pastor at New Christ Memorial Church.
- The *American Idol* runner-up in 2006, Katharine McPhee, attended Notre Dame High School in Sherman Oaks.
- In the 1980s, Rock guitar legend Eddie Van Halen managed Al' n Ed's Auto Sound Store in Studio City.
- The lead singer of *Incubus*, Brandon Boyd, graduated from Calabasas High School and attended Moorpark College.
- It is believed that Rap music started in Woodland Hills at Taft High School.
- Tupac Shakur lived in Calabasas at one time.
- Easy E's playhouse was also located in Calabasas.
- Rapper, producer, and entrepreneur Dr. Dre lived at one time in Woodland Hills.
- Ice Cube called the Valley home.
- Bruno Mars once owned a secluded Studio City mansion.
- Miley Cyrus has owned at least three houses in the Valley, one in Hidden Hills.
- The Jonas Brothers grew up in Toluca Lake.

And then there's the California State University Northridge (CSUN) music connection. The college offers several undergraduate and graduate music degrees. As a result, CSUN alumni include some familiar names, including:

- Paula Abdul, who was a cheerleader at Van Nuys High School.
- Guitarist Andy Summers of the *Police* studied the classical guitar at CSUN.
- The keyboardist from *Human Drama,* Mark Balderas, was born in Encino.
- Daryl Dragon, the lead of the group *The Captain and Tennille*, studied piano at CSUN.
- Renowned session bassist Leland Sklar studied at CSUN. He used his talents to record with many music greats, including Jackson Brown, Linda Ronstadt, James Taylor, Phil Collins, Carole King, and others.

- Jim Pons, bass guitarist and singer for *The Turtles*, Frank Zappa, and *Mothers of Invention*, also attended CSUN.
- Mike Elizondo, the legendary record producer for groups and musicians like Eminem, Alanis Morrissette, and Pink, was born and raised in Pacoima.
- Michael Jackson lived in Encino, as noted above.
- Singer/songwriter Bonnie Raitt was born and raised in Burbank.
- Grammy-winning jazz singer Al Jarreau lived in Encino before he died.

The Valley also became known in the 1960s as the place to discover new music. And it's still got that reputation today and for good reason. Many local bands started their careers in the Valley at various local hot spots. One, called the Cobalt Café, was located in Canoga Park. Owner Dave Politi, a Valley native, says he based his club on New York City's trendy and hip CBGBs. Many bands got their start there over the years, including *Jimmy Eat World, AFI, Less Than Jake, Eve 6, Reel Big Fish, Save Ferris, Avenged Sevenfold, New Found Glory, Something Corporate, Rx Bandits.*

Another prominent Valley music venue is The Canyon in Agoura Hills. This place is still going strong today due to its reputation for booking top name bands interspersed with entertaining tribute acts. The Canyon's opened in 2000 and quickly became the place to see all kinds of music, from rock and country to jazz and even blues. Some of the bands you read about above played at The Canyon, including *Hoobastank* and *OneRepublic*, along with Jackson Browne, *Heart, Velvet Revolver*, Willie Nelson, Ben Harper, Dave Davies, B.B. King, and others.

The Cowboy Palace Saloon is a historic music joint and dive bar in Chatsworth. This place has live country music and pool tables because what dive bar would be complete without pool tables?

Then there's the Valley Performing Arts Center at CSUN, where students hold concerts alongside well-known artists in all forms of music. And the Alex Theatre in Glendale offers a variety of adult world music, symphonies, and musical.

Tip #6 Famous Movies About the Valley

The music scene is not the only creative outlet in the Valley. Thousands of movies and TV shows have been—and still are—filmed here. Because the Valley isn't quite like its more glamorous neighbors, Hollywood executives have used the rural feel in many Western shows, including *Bonanza, The Lone Ranger*, and *The Outlaw*.

But Westerns weren't the only genre. In fact, some of your favorite movies from the '80s on up are not only filmed in the Valley but feature the area almost like one of the leading characters. For instance, in *Once Upon a Time in Hollywood*, the historic Mexican restaurant Casa Vega. Once you see the place in person, you'll notice it as the background of a crucial scene between Rick Dalton (Leonardo DiCaprio) and Cliff Booth (Brad Pitt) So it's safe to say that actors Leonardo DiCaprio and Brad Pitt have been there. The proof can be seen on the big screen. However, even when not working there, many celebs have been known to dine there.

The Hollywood executives behind iconic films like *Back to the Future* used the quiet neighborhood of Arleta as the home of hero Marty McFly. You'll find Marty's House on Roslyndale Ave in front of the Arleta DMV.

Along Sherman Way, you'll find an old, abandoned theater used in the opening of *Boogie Nights* as The Hot Traxx Disco. And the *Cobra Kai Dojo* in *The Karate Kid* is actually an abandoned building in the NoHo Arts District.

When he needed a location for the junkyard Monster Joe's in *Pulp Fiction*, Quinten Tarantino turned to A & R Auto Dismantlers in Sun Valley. And remember the Crown Pawn Shop in that movie? Well, that was real too. When not being used in films, anyone can pawn their valuables for cash there.

Established in 1946, The Smokehouse restaurant in Burbank has welcomed numerous stars through its doors over the years. Being close to Warner Brothers studios makes the Smokehouse a popular place for celebrities and producers to meet, eat and make deals. The place is so famous that actor George Clooney actually chose the name for his production company.

The real house where Jackson Maine (Bradley Cooper) lived in *A Star is Born* is actually located in Calabasas. You might remember seeing it as the backdrop in the final scene. Does a single-story mid-century property ring a bell?

Another mid-century modern house was used in the Tom Ford film, *A Single Man*. Located in Glendale and built in 1949, besides being rented out as a location, the home is listed on the National Register of Historic Places.

The Mulholland Drive Canyon is so famous that it has a David Lynch film named after it. But even more, many celebrities have lived or do live in the area, including Marlon Brando, Jack Nicholson, John Lennon, Madonna, Roman Polanski, Bruce Willis, Demi Moore, and David Lynch himself.

When you see a particular office building in Van Nuys, you might think you've left the Valley and are now in Scranton, PA. That's because the simple, gray office building was used in *The Office* as the location of the fictional Dunder Mifflin company. In real life, the building is the home of Chandler Valley Center Studios.

So, now you understand. The Valley is famous in its own right. So famous, there are 24 movies that are actually based on the area. Yes, the suburban tract homes, strip malls, and asphalt roads make the perfect location for some of our most beloved storylines. And for some movies, the Valley is not just a location, but the Valley itself is central to the storyline. The list is from newest to oldest. Ready? Here we go:

- *2 Days in the Valley*
- *A Cinderella Story*
- *Bad News Bears*
- *Boogie Nights*
- *Crash*
- *Dancing at the Blue Iguana*
- *Down in the Valley*
- *E.T. The Extra-Terrestrial*
- *Earth Girls are Easy*
- *Encino Man*
- *Every Which Way but Loose*
- *Foxes*
- *La Bamba*
- *Magnolia*
- *Plan 9 From Outer Space*
- *Safe*
- *San Fernando Valley*
- *The Karate Kid*
- *The Karate Kid Part II*
- *The Karate Kid Part III*
- *The Lonely Lady*

- *The Sandlot*
- *The Sandlot II*
- *Valley Girl*

Okay, now you know some of the films about the Valley, but what about those made in the Valley where the landscape is only a background? There are too many to dd them all here, but some you've probably seen or, at the very least, heard about include:

- *A Cinderella Story*
- *Adventures of Superman*
- *Any Which Way You Can*
- *Apache*
- *Big Bad Mama*
- *Bill & Ted's Bogus Journey*
- *Bucky Larson: Born to Be a Star*
- *CHIPs*
- *Cobra Kai*
- *Dark Victory*
- *Deadly Prey*
- *Death Race 2000*
- *Doctor Dolittle*
- *Earth Girls are Easy*
- *Erin Brockovich*
- *Every Which Way but Loose*
- *Fast Times at Ridgemont High*
- *Frankenstein*
- *Joan of Arc*
- *Lassie Come Home*
- *Leprechaun 2*
- *Lethal Weapon*
- *Manson*
- *Night of the Creeps*
- *Paris, Texas*
- *Phantasm*
- *Phantasm II*

- *Planet of Dinosaurs*
- *Pork Chop Hill*
- *Psycho*
- *Punch-Drunk Love*
- *Starlet*
- *Starving in Suburbia*
- *State of the Union*
- *Terminator 2: Judgement Day*
- *The Adams Family*
- *The Bad News Bears*
- *The Bad News Bears in Breaking Training*
- *The Bad News Bears in Breaking Training*
- *The Birth of a Nation*
- *The End of Violence*
- *The Girl Next Door*
- *The Gold Rush*
- *The Good Earth*
- *The Grapes of Wrath*
- *The Great Dictator*
- *The Karate Kid*
- *The Mark of Zorro*
- *The Men*
- *The Quick Gun*
- *The Roommates*
- *The Runaways*
- *The Tin Star*
- *The Toolbox Murders*
- *They Live by Night*

Another piece of Valley movie trivia has to do with the Panorama Theater in Panorama City. But it's not about a film location. This time, it's about the location of where films are shown.

The Panorama Theater opened on December 20, 1949, with the film classic, *Always Leave Them Laughing*. Back then, the film stars Milton Berle, and Virginia Mayo actually made a personal appearance at the film's opening. It closed in 1994 and now serves as a church for the Brazilian-based Universal Church of the Kingdom of God.

Panorama City itself has an impressive list of actors, musicians, athletes, and artists who grew up there, including:

- Actor Kirk Cameron
- Actor Mark-Paul Gosselaar
- Actress Candace Cameron Bure
- Actress Meagan Good
- Artist Sara Velas
- Baseball player Steve Wapnick
- Boxer José Benavidez,
- Major League Baseball Player Giancarlo Stanton
- Musician Mike Shinoda
- New York Yankees pitcher Zack Britton.
- Olympic Volleyball player David Smith
- Rapper Hopsin
- Terry Gilliam from *Monty Python* fame

Will this trend continue? Stay tuned!

Tip #7 The Porn Capital of the World

Did you know that the Valley was once known as The Porn Capital of the World? Here's how that happened:

In the beginning, the porn industry could be found in Los Angeles, San Francisco, and New York. But by the 1970s, the Valley became the central location for porn. Speculation is that low rents for locations combined with access to Hollywood and talent made the Valley the perfect choice.

Porn in the Valley grew to become a multibillion-dollar industry. A significant number of adult videos and magazines were made in the Valley. The dirty little secret created nicknames like Porn Valley, Silicone Valley, or the San Pornando Valley.

If you want to know what the Valley was like back then, watch *Boogie Nights*. And HBO's Pornucopia shares some interesting facts about the Valley and porn. For example, it's hard to imagine that in the suburbs of Los Angeles, almost 90% of porn made in the USA was filmed or produced in the Valley.

By the mid-2000s, the growing amount of free content on the Internet put a big dent in the porn industry, causing revenues to drop. Makes sense. Why should someone pay when they can watch for free?

Tip #8 The Northridge Earthquake

Anyone who lived in Northridge in 1994 remembers the earthquake that struck on January 17. It measured 6.7 and caused serious injury to more than 1,500 people, while 57 people died that day. Houses were found to be unfit to live in, which made almost 67,000 people homeless for a time. Major freeways collapsed or were server damaged which caused some to close. Even after a few days, homes and businesses were still without electricity or water.

The quake could be felt in Beverly Hills, where I lived in the guesthouse of some well-off friends. My little home was right outside a swimming pool. I'll never forget picking up my dog Blondie and opening the door to witness huge waves crashing onto the patio.

My parents still lived in the Northridge ranch-style home where I grew up. When I finally got a hold of them, I found out that they were fine, but the house was severely damaged. They spent the next two years living in their bedroom while the house was repaired. Luckily, my dad had purchased earthquake insurance. Unfortunately, when I drove out to check on them, the Valley looked like a war zone. I'd never witnessed anything like it and hope I never do again.

The other quake that rattled me and thousands of others away happened in 1971 when I was in junior high school. Then, the 6.2 magnitude Sylmar quake rocked our Northridge house with a vengeance. I remember grabbing my dog Siesta and huddling in the doorway with my dad, mom, brother, and sister. A doorway was believed to be the safest place to ride out a quake back then, but that is no longer the case. Now, experts say the safest spot is under a desk or table.

The quake caused lots of damage to homes, especially those built directly under the Faultline. Plus, roads and freeways closed while bridges and hospitals collapsed. Even Holmes Junior High received so much damage that we didn't have to go to school for weeks. Needless to say, the quake left an indelible mark on my young life.

So now you know what to do if you're visiting the area and feel the earth shake. Just ride it out under a table or desk.

Chapter Review

- Called the Valley by locals, the area's rich history began with Native American tribes living off the land until 1769, when the Spanish discovered it.

- The Valley has been a haven for celebrities since the early days of the entertainment industry.
- Besides setting up her Desilu Studios in the Valley, Lucille Ball and Ricky Ricardo owned a ranch there too.
- There are many movies made about the Valley and even more shot in the Valley. Valley Girl, anyone?
- There are several places where you can see celebrities in their day-to-day life.

Chapter 2: Not to Miss Secret Gems

There are so many interesting and unusual places in the Valley to explore, including:

Tip #9 The Brady Bunch House

Did you know the popular television show *The Brady Bunch* has roots in the Valley? Well, it does. The family home featured in the hit from the late 1960s to the 1970s is located in Studio City.

I remember seeing Susan Marie Olsen at lunch in the tearoom at Bullock's Sherman Oaks, a swanky place that was extremely popular back then. Cindy, the actress who played the youngest of the six children, looked exactly the same in person as she did on my family's little black and white TV set. Yes, we were one of the only families in our community that didn't own a color set. And even the black and white one was rented. Mom and Dad had their priorities, and television viewing was not one of them.

Once you see the actual home where the Brady tribe lived in the TV world, you'll recognize it. The home's interior scenes were shot at Paramount Studios.

In 2018, HGTV bought the home to feature in a new show, *A Very Brady Renovation*. The show was all authentically renovating and decorating the interior and exterior of the Sherman Oaks home, so it's a carbon copy of the original TV ranch home. In addition, the grown-up Brady kids appeared on the show and shared their personal memories of growing up in the public eye.

The actual house has never stopped attracting Brady Bunch fans. And while they come to see it, many are not aware of the following:

- The White House may be the most photographed in the nation, but the Brady home comes in second.
- The original house was a three-bedroom, three-bath split-level 2,477 square foot ranch-style home featuring a huge backyard. The Northridge home where I grew up also had a big backyard. I remember playing for hours in what I referred to as my own private Eden.
- The home has a 1970s vintage vibe, even though it was built in 1959.
- HGTV bought the home in a bidding war. Former NSYNC member Lance Bass wanted it, and so did Marcia, Marcia, Marcia, the Brady's oldest sister, played by actress Maureen McCormick.
- All six Brady kids were tasked with finding memorabilia from way back when. Many items were found and returned.

As of right now, The Brady Bunch house is not open to the public. But no one's stopping you from taking a selfie in front of it! You could even use that photo for your Christmas Card. Here's the address: 11222 Dilling Street, Studio City.

Tip #10 Woodland Hills' Cylinder House

If you ever find yourself on Canoga Avenue south of Ventura Boulevard, be sure to look up. You'll see what some say looks like an alien or something out of this world. You can't miss it, even though the unusual home is located on a forested hilltop. It's called the Al Struckus House, owned and built by a man who worked as an engineer. There's no doubt his engineering knowledge came in handy for this unique project he undertook.

It's not surprising to learn that the Struckus house was designed by a famous Modern architect named Bruce Goff. However, it holds the distinction of being the last design he completed before his death in 1982.

The Struckus house was built on a small lot on Saltillo Street, and you'll know it when you see a building made of six interlacing tube-like cylinders. The center is four stories high, surrounded by the other cylinders. The materials used include glass tiles, stucco, and redwood.

Unfortunately, there are no tours, so you can't visit the inside of Struckus' architectural work of art. If you could, you'd be amazed at the vertical art gallery, which just happens to be suspended above the indoor pool. You'd also find circular skylights inside, with curved windows and closets.

Still, there's nothing stopping you from taking pictures of this unique property, at least from the outside. So post them on your social media pages and see what interesting comments you receive!

Tip #11 Original Batmobile was created in the Valley

Zap! Boom! Bang! The 1966 Batmobile from the TV series *Batman* was created and built in fifteen days for $15,000 by George Barris of Barris Kustoms. The famous vehicle sat for years in the showroom of Barris Kustoms, which took up practically an entire block on Riverside Drive in North Hollywood since the day George "King of the Kustomizers" Barris set up shop there more than 60 years ago.

Barris Kustom built the first Batmobile based on the concept of a 1955 Lincoln Futura car. The original car, used in the Batman TV series, sold at auction in 2013 for more than $4 million. Besides the Batmobile, George also created the Munster Koach and several award-winning vehicles.

The company is also famous for its custom roadsters named the Barrister, a favorite of the Hollywood elite, including Sammy Davis Jr. and Liberace.

After Barris died in 2015, his family kept Barris Kustom open on Riverside Drive. But it was never the same, and the family finally decided that a full custom shop was no longer practical, especially since most family members had relocated from the area.

Tip #12 The 94th Aero Squadron restaurant at Van Nuys Airport

Next to the Van Nuys Airport, you'll find the 94th Aero Squadron restaurant that serves delicious American food. It looks like a French farmhouse from the outside until you notice all the old American Jeeps on the front lawn. Inside, you'll find aviation relics, including piles of old-time photographs and framed photos on the walls alongside antique uniforms and other wartime artifacts from WW1 and WWII.

Hearing planes as they take off and land at the small airport next door just adds to the ambiance. The restaurant also has banquet rooms, perfect for events. This is the dream of local David Tallichet, who was inspired by his own experience in the Army during World War II.

Tip #13 Remnants of the Cold War

Located off Mulholland Drive above Encino, you'll find San Vicente Mountain Park, a one-of-a-kind reclamation project that might be the most unusual in the US. During the Cold War, this place, with its breathtaking views, was actually a United States military base. Known as LA-96C, from 1956 to 1968, this base was one of sixteen in the Los Angeles area that included launch sites for Nike-Ajax supersonic anti-aircraft missiles. Then, in 1996, the Santa Monica Mountain National Recreation Area opened to the public as a park.

You'll find many displays that pay homage to the area's historical past when you visit. Some call the park a solemn reminder of the destruction war causes. To others, it's the perfect example of what can be created in the absence of war. But no matter what you call it, you can't beat those views!

Tip #14 Kayak the LA River

You can visit and even kayak the LA River from approximately May to September. During most of the year, public access to the river is limited, but the Mountains Recreation and Conservation Authority allows public use of two designated areas during the summer months. That's when the LA River comes alive with people walking, bird watching, fishing, and using non-motorized/steerable boats like kayaks.

The Sepulveda Basin River Recreation Zone located in Encino spreads a couple of miles from Balboa Boulevard to just west of Woodley Avenue. Anyone can steer a non-motorized kayak or canoe for free. However, if needed, there are several places to rent.

To get to the Sepulveda Basin Recreation Zone, the approximate address for your GPS is 16212 Burbank Boulevard, Encino, CA 91436. The area is clearly marked, so you'll know it when you get there.

Tip #15 The Rancho Equestrian District

The Rancho Equestrian District in Burbank is heaven for those who love the equestrian life. The Los Angeles Equestrian Center is smack dab in the middle of the district and is full of events, from horse shows to polo matches and more. The facility also offers horse facilities for those who want to board their horse(s) and utilize the riding amenities.

You'll find residents on horseback riding down the area's tree-lined streets. It is perhaps the closest thing to rural living you can find near Hollywood and downtown Los Angeles.

Tip #16 The California Institute of Abnormalarts

On Burbank Blvd in North Hollywood, just past the body shops and auto parts warehouses, you'll find the California Institute of Abnormalarts (CIA). Enter, and you'll find yourself submerged in an alternate universe.

The brainchild of actor-screenwriter Carl Crew, who has since become known as the Barnum of Burbank Blvd., and his partner Robert Ferguson, the hosts offbeat underground bands, bizarre performance art shows, movie screenings, burlesque, puppet shows, stand-up comedy, freak shows—just about any unusual performance can be seen here.

Plus, you'll find sideshow memorabilia that the owners have collected over the years. But the venue itself could be considered performance art, painted in brash circus colors with crypto taxidermy displays next to weird oddities and hoaxes, including the head of Sasquatch, a fairy skeleton, a Fiji mermaid from Fiji, and the preserved corpse of a circus performer complete in the clown makeup and costume he wore before he died in 1912.

Tip #17 Farmer's Markets

With its history as an agricultural center, Farmer's Markets in the Valley feature the freshest, locally grown fruits and vegetables and more. Here are the ones not to miss:

- Studio City Farmer's Market
  Every week, vendors set up on Ventura Place, and locals come to shop for fresh fruits and vegetables along with artesian breads, olive oils, honey, and more. This market has a real community vibe.
- The Burbank Farmers Market
  One of the oldest Farmer's Markets in Southern California, you can shop for locally grown fruit and veggies alongside olive oil, cheese, salsa, hummus, freshly baked breads, and pastries. If you want some fresh egg from Gama Farms, you'l have to wait in line, just sayin'.
- The Northridge Farmer's Market
  This family-friendly Farmers Market is held on Wednesday evenings, and it's always busy. Located in the parking lot of the Northridge Mall, shop and dine the food vendors while you listen to live music.

Tip #18 Iliad Bookshop

If used books are your thing, head to North Hollywood's Iliad Bookstore. This unique store is one of the biggest used bookstores in the Los Angeles area, with more than 150,000 titles on its shelves. While there, you'll probably bump into one of the store's cats lounging on one of the comfy sofas. You'll also enjoy the music and the free parking. If the shop looks familiar, it's because it's been used as a location in countless movies and television shows. So, be sure to take a selfie while you're there. Maybe get one of the cats in it too!

Tip #19 Cruising Van Nuys Blvd

Back in the day, Wednesday night in the Valley was known as cruise night on Van Nuys Boulevard. Cruising Van Nuys dates back to the 1950s with the Valley's popular Bob's Big Boy restaurant that opened as a drive-in along Van Nuys. It quickly became a car show of its own, with people lining up to receive carhop service.

Then, in the 1970s, Van Nuys became popular with young people enjoying their freedom after the worst of the Vietnam war was over. Everyone met at the south end of Van Nuys at a strip mall to show off their wheels and hang out with friends. Many of the cruisers were low riders, while others were classic cars.

Tip #20 Anthony C. Beilenson Park

The Japanese cherry blossom trees at Anthony C. Beilenson Park are sort of famous. They were gifted to the Valley by a Japanese-based company and planted back in 1992. They line the entrance of Lake Balboa with pink blooms from late March to early April.

But don't worry if you can't make it during the spring. There's something at the 80-acre park for everyone in your family. Picnic anyone? There's the perfect area for that with barbeques. Take a spin on any of the park's bike trails. You can fish or even fly fish at the lake. There's a workout area, a children's play area, or you can rent a paddleboat for some fun on the lake. Dogs are allowed, too, as long as they stay on a leash.

Tip #21 Academy of TV Arts and Sciences

Located in North Hollywood's NoHo Arts District, this not-for-profit organization was founded in 1946 and currently has about 20,000 members. This is the place that shapes what you watch on your TV every night and is the organization behind the annual Primetime Emmy Awards honoring your favorite television personalities.

You may wonder why it is a nonprofit? Because the foundation provides resources for up-and-coming talent too. In fact, many prominent writers, producers, executives, documentarians, and others in the industry are all part of the foundation's alumni.

Tip #22 Iguana Vintage Clothing and American Vintage

This clothing and costume shop probably started the trend of recycling at its three locations, two of which are in the Valley, Sherman Oaks, and North Hollywood. What you'll find there is unique, one-of-a-kind vintage and retro fashions for men, women, and children. Voted the best vintage clothing store year after year, Iguana is also embraced by the LA design community.

Tip #23 Psychic Eye Bookstore

With two locations in Sherman Oaks, this eclectic shop offers New Age books and music, metaphysical supplies, and psychic consultations. Since opening in 1985, the Psychic Eye Book Shop holds the distinction of having the largest collection of New and Old Age books. It is also the place to go in the Valley if you are looking for metaphysical gifts. Just entering one of the stores will make you feel spiritual.

The stores are filled with tarot cards, books, instructional magazines, and other psychic artifacts,

Plus, its professional psychic consultants are available by phone, in-person, or can be booked for group events.

Tip #24 Leonis Adobe Museum

The Leonis Adobe Museum is part monument and part museum, located in Calabasas. Located in the middle of Calabasas Creek Park, this is the place to take a look back into the history of ranch life in California in late 1880. You'll also find a replica of a Chumash village, the Calabasas Jail, and other elements from the same time period, as well as the Plummer House, which was moved there in 1983 and has since been beautifully restored.

The adobe was originally owned by a colorful character at the time, Miguel Leonis, aka the "King of Calabasas." Leonis was one of the many French-speaking immigrants that settled here. Although he could not read or write, Leonis claimed about 11,000 prime acres. Imagine what that would be worth now?

Today, both the adobe and Plummer House are open for tours.

Tip #25 Small Herd of Texas Longhorn Cattle

Believe it or not, there's a small herd of Texas Longhorns that live in Calabasas at the Leonis Adobe Monument. As beloved ambassadors, they are an important part of the museum experience, representing the yard of an authentic ranch in the 1880s.

You don't have to visit Leonis Adobe to see them because they are big-time YouTube stars where a museum guide introduces each member of the herd. But if you want to see them in person, you're in luck. Throughout the year, there are several programs at the museum where visitors can see them and feed the herd, all to show how important ranch animals were to settlers.

Few people know about the role Longhorn cattle played in the history of California. They were brought here by Spanish explorers and missionaries, including Father Serra, the founder of Californian missions. They were used as food and for trade—think boots and shoes—and were extremely important in the economic development of the Valley, as well as the entire golden state. Yet, somehow their part in Valley and state history has been all but forgotten.

Tip #26 Woodley Park Cricket Field and Archery Range

Yes, the Valley has its own cricket complex located inside Woodley Park. The Leo Magnus Cricket Complex (LMCC) was built by the Valley's West Indian cricket community. The first two fields opened in 1980, with two more added in the following decade.

The United States of America Cricket Association holds trials there. At one of those trials, it is believed that Mick Jagger of the Rolling Stones, who is an admitted fan of the sport, stopped by to watch.

There's also an archery range at Woodley Park, which opened in 1984. The facility is run by a group called Woodley Park Archers. They offer classes in the sport at the facility, which has both short and long ranges and is lit in the evenings.

The range is used as a training facility for the Olympic Games. But you don't have to be a pro to use it. You can join a league and practice there.

Tip #27 San Fernando Valley RC Flyers Apollo 11 Field

It's an impressive sight when you see radio-controlled model airplanes overhead. And here, enthusiasts from all over the world gather to show off their talents. More than 400 modelers, as they're called, are part of the club, but anyone can join the fun. They even offer lessons from instructor pilots. So even if you're not interested in learning about the sport, you'll be impressed watching the giant scale pylons and helicopters in the sky.

Tip #28 Los Angeles Pet Memorial Park in Calabasas

The Los Angeles Pet Memorial Park is the place to lay to rest beloved, furry family members. Founded by celebrity veterinarian Dr. Eugene Jones in 1928, the cemetery sits on a quiet hillside off the Ventura freeway. Besides a place to remember family pets, it is known for being the final resting place for many animal stars, including:

- Tawny, one of the MGM Lions, Jiggs
- "Cheetah" from Tarzan
- Pete the Pup from "Our Gang"
- Topper – the trusty steed of Hopalong Cassidy

And as the final resting spot for many animals of celebrities, including:

- Rudolph Valentino's loyal Alsatian Doberman
- *Kabar*, Mae West's monkey
- *Boogie*, Humphrey Bogart, and Lauren Bacall's champagne cocker spaniel
- Droopy, and *Muggins,* Jimmy Durante's Irish Setter

Anyone can visit the cemetery and see the celebrity gravesites. It is also touching to see family pets remembered with unique markers.

Tip #29 Asanebo Restaurant

There are several excellent sushi restaurants in the Valley, so many, in fact, that part of Ventura Boulevard in Sherman Oaks has been named Sushi Row. Asanebo Restaurant stands out from the rest, serving fresh, delicious sushi that looks like a work of art. The recipient of two Michelin stars, guests can choose from three menus that range in price from $85-$200. Not bad for some of the absolute best tasting and looking sushi in the area. For example, picture this: white shrimp topped with gold flakes or digging into a conch shell while it's flaming. The restaurant itself is the perfect backdrop for the artful dishes it serves. The whimsical, sparse space uses Hello Kitty dolls as décor and the owner, Chef Tetsuya, is quite the character himself. Visit, and you'll see (and taste) for yourself!

Tip #30 Eclectica Vintage

This unique shop located in North Hollywood has the best vintage and antique items you'll find anywhere. We're taking hip clothing, cool furniture, funky housewares, one-of-a-kind collectibles, and fine art, all curated by Mike Fitch, a veteran of Hollywood costuming and set design. He opened the store in 2010 and continues to add new items all the time. So you never know what you'll find at Eclectica Vintage.

Tip #31 Bob's Big Boy

Did you know that the Bob's Big Boy restaurant chain got its start in the Valley? Well, it did, thanks to Glendale resident Robert C. Wian. His first restaurant, a humble 10-stool hamburger joint called Bob's

Pantry, opened in 1936. Wian used the $300 cash made from selling his car, a DeSoto Roadster, as a down payment. Today, there are 77 Bob's Big Boy restaurants in the United States, and another 279 can be found in Japan.

The name Bob's Big Boy came later after the signature double-patty hamburger was added to the menu. The logo of the boy in red suspenders actually came from a six-year-old customer. A professional animator originally created it from Warner Brothers in exchange for a hamburger.

Fast forward to 1967. That's the year Wian cashed out and sold his restaurant chain to Marriott for a whopping $7 million. Today, the Valley is home to three of the original Bob's Big Boy restaurants. So yes, you can still enjoy one of the chain's famous burgers in Glendale, Burbank, or North Hollywood. Plus, the Big Boy fiberglass mascot stands proudly in front of the Burbank restaurant, so be sure to get a picture with him to share with your followers.

Tip #32 Valley Inn Martini Bar

You'll think you traveled back in time when you enter the Valley Inn Martini Bar. This landmark restaurant that serves a mean Martini and the most delicious American fare opened in 1947 and has maintained the style of that era ever since. The bar is even older. It was crafted by hand in the 1800s.

Did someone say comfort food? It's here in the form of salads, sandwiches, steaks, and all the comfort food you need. Feel better now?

Tip #33 TreePeople

TreePeople is a nonprofit organization dedicated to advocating for a sustainable urban ecosystem. How do they do it? Through education and advocacy with volunteerism at its core. Oh, and there are trees—many trees at the organization's main site on Mulholland Drive.

Started by a teenager more than 40 years ago, today, the organization has inspired locals to plant millions of trees in and around greater Los Angeles. The real work takes place offsite in various communities where volunteers plant trees and educate the public on their importance. TreePeople also prides itself on influencing government agencies to support healthy cities.

Tip #34 Fryman Canyon Park

All 122-acres of Fryman Canyon Park can be enjoyed in Sherman Oaks. Located on Mulholland Drive, this park has access to some of the best hiking trails around. And not just any trails. We're talking hikes with spectacular views, beautiful canyons, trickling streams, a rainforest, and much more.

One of the trails crosses the entire park and connects to canyons in the Santa Monica Mountains. Even your dog can join the fun, as long as they remain leashed. The trails are filled with wildflowers in the spring, and the weather is perfect. Both are open all year long for hikers, runners, and anyone who loves mother nature.

Tip #35 Sepulveda Basin Wildlife Reserve

The Sepulveda Wildlife Reserve offers a glimpse of how the Valley looked more than 100 years ago. The 225 bird-friendly acres make a ort of birdy playground with everything our feathered friends need o survive. It still provides a haven for millions of birds traveling to ınd from Central America and Mexico, as well as hiking trails for ıumans. There are also special events held there as well as guided ıikes.

ıuckily, this important Wildlife Reserve was spared progress as the √alley welcomed more and more residents over the years. Home to √ildlife Lake, a small pond, and a trickling creek, the reserve's ▾ater, along with the variety of habitats, attracts all kinds of birds. 3ut, of course, what you'll see depends on the time of year you visit. ▾e're talking Canadian geese, owls, ducks, warblers, flycatchers, ;horebirds, hummingbirds, kingbirds, orioles, grosbeaks, swallows, ınd more. You'll even see some birds of prey like hawks flying ▾verhead looking for their next meal while species like the Blue 3rosbeak use the refuge for breeding, one of the only breeding sites ´or these beautiful creatures in the United States. As you can ımagine, this is the place for bird watchers who get to see more than ?00 species here.

Tip #36 Landmark Van Nuys City Hall

The Los Angeles City Hall has a mini-me that can be found in the √alley. That's right, the building that has been used in countless ımovies like Superman has a miniature doppelganger called Van Nuys City Hall. Built in 1932, this striking Art Deco-Moderne ɔuilding with its central tower topped by a concert dome was ıamed a Historic-Cultural Monument in 1968. Many of the ɔuilding's features are original, from the lobby made of marble, the ;entral stairway, the doors to the main entrance, the hardware, and ?ven a mail chute made of bronze.

Originally, the wings of this architecturally significant building wer split between a hospital in and the Police Department, including th Municipal Court and jail. However, as the population in the Valley increased in the 1950s and 1960s, both the hospital and Police Department were relocated, and the entire space was remodeled fo City offices.

I remember visiting once during grade school with my best friend's father, who was a local attorney. Even at a young age, the building itself struck me as something unusual and important, especially juxtaposed to its surroundings. Now the area is a bit run down, but the building stands tall as a reminder of the beautiful architecture of the past.

Tip #37 World's Longest Mural

On Coldwater Canyon in North Hollywood, you'll find the Great Wall of Los Angeles, aka the History of California. This has the distinction of being one of the biggest murals in the world. Yes, one of the biggest murals in the entire world can be found in the Valley! How big, you ask? The mural stands over thirteen feet tall and stretches out over a half-mile. What's on the mural, you ask? California's history through the 1960s.

You'll find vibrant scenarios of the events and people important in the creation of the Valley depicted, included from the birth of the Valley to the cultural influence of Native American Indians, along with scenes depicting African, Latino, Asian, and Jewish Americans and more who all had a hand in creating the California culture we know today. The themes that are highlighted on the Great Wall include issues such as immigration, women's rights, racism, gay and lesbian, and more. The mural itself was painted by teams of young residents supervised by local artists. The primary concept came from Chicana Judith F. Baca, a celebrated local muralist who worked with the Social and Public Art Resource Center (SPARC) on making her vision a reality.

Tip #38 Tonga Hut

Don't miss visiting the Tonga Hut in North Hollywood if you're into Tiki culture. The oldest surviving tiki bar in all of Los Angeles opened in 1934. Tiki Bars were all the rage back then, thanks to the lifting of Prohibition. The trend in the golden state started with two separate entrepreneurs, each with the bright idea of opening a small neighborhood bar with tropical drinks and décor. Both bars quickly became known for strong rum drinks, including the mai tai, which means out of this world in Tahitian. And that was the birth of Tiki culture here.

Ace and Ed Libby took over the management of the Tonga Hut in 1958 and made it the cool joint that it is today with its delicious fruity drinks and tropical décor featuring lava-rock fountains. Plus, the jukebox adds even more ambiance with music from Johnny Cash to Kiss interspersed with some Hawaiian favorites. The interior features just what you'd think—dim lighting accented with a driftwood sculpture and a huge map of the Polynesian islands to set the stage, along with leather benches and curved booths and a cozy fireplace.

And for those yearning to go down in history for doing something noble, accept the Tonga Hut challenge, and in the course of a year, try all 78 drinks. Your name will be added to the Grog Log, and you will become a member of the Loyal Order of the Drooling Bastard. Add that to your resume.

Tip #39 The Tarzan Museum

You might ask, what does Tarzan have to do with the Valley? That's a very good question, and the answer is everything since the fictional tale about Tarzan was written by a Valley resident. Yes, author Edgar Rice Burroughs lived in a ranch house in a community that is now named after his most famous hero.

The mission of the Tarzan Museum is to nurture and enrich Tarzana residents and visitors with the unique neighborhood's rich history. As such, the museum is filled with an ever-growing collection of memorabilia related to the town. In addition, you'll find interesting documents, books, and photos related to the town's famous namesake, the jungle hero Tarzan.

Included in the collection is a mission bell with links to Marlon Brando. This is actually one of the most popular pieces of history on display which originally hung at a large Spanish hacienda in Coldwater Canyon. The red-tiled roof estate was built in the late 1920s or early 1930s and later owned by a famous actor in the 1960s.

The Museum is located at the Tarzana Community and Cultural Center. This one-of-a-kind gathering offers a wide variety of community events and activities besides the Tarzan Museum. It's a popular place for outdoor weddings, garden parties, filming, picnics, anniversary, and birthday celebrations. It's also a great place to relax in the lush, colorful garden vignettes on a warm summer day.

Tip #40 Shopping

Being part of Los Angeles, the home of movie stars and reality celebrities, looking your best is of utmost importance in the Valley. So, as you can imagine, shopping is a fine art here, especially with all the celebrity stylists and costume designers who work here. You can shop like one of them at any of the following:

Malls

The shopping mall was not invented in the Valley, but it was perfected here. As a result, just about anything you're looking for can be found at the mall. Even more, the outdoor malls in the Valley make the perfect gathering place for a variety of reasons. As a result, meeting at the mall takes on new heights in the Valley. Here's a list of where to go:

- **Westfield Fashion Square in Sherman Oaks**

For the high-end mall experience, go to Westfield Fashion Square in Sherman Oaks. You'll find department stores like Bloomingdale's and Macy's, Pottery Barn, Williams Sonoma, Sephora, and about 130 others there. It's rather small in size, making shopping there a more intimate affair, especially if you're into exclusive designers. The food court is also small, but there's certainly something for everyone. Santa visits every year for photos, and even four-legged family members can join the party.

- **Westfield Topanga & The Village in Canoga Park**

The Westfield Topanga & The Village is much larger than its sister in Sherman Oaks that you just read about. Shopping options here are plentiful, with more than 300 stores, including Nordstrom's and Neiman Marcus. This mall is the perfect place to shop plein air for everything from the hippest styles at Planet Funk to stylish shoes at Aldo or a real treasure from Tiffany & Co. And this mall doesn't have an ordinary food court. At the Village, you'll find some of the best restaurants, lounges, and bars. The mall's entertainment options aren't bad either, with movie theaters and more. Along with Santa, the Easter Bunny visits every year for fun and photos with the family.

- **Americana at Brand in Glendale**

Built at the cost of $400 million, Americana at Brand is more than a shopping center. Besides the usual shopping, dining, and entertainment options at this mall, you can also call it home. The complex sits on more than fifteen picturesque acres featuring style and beauty events, cultural, food, and wine celebrations, and an 18-screen theater. I once put on an event there myself on Black Friday featuring one of the hero dogs from 9/11. Shoppers were invited to get their picture taken with the well-trained white lab who was in New York after the tragedy working with police, fire, and rescue workers. Mason, the hero dog, was a big hit!

- **Northridge Fashion Center**

Unlike the malls mentioned above, the Northridge Fashion Center is independently owned and family-run. Opening in 1971, this mall still offers the very best in retail with more than 170 stores. Here, you'll find items for the whole family, including your favorite national brands like H&M, Apple, Pandora, Starbucks, and much, much more. There are also outside dining options and movie theatres. Oh, and here, your dog can meet the Easter Bunny for spring photo opportunities. Growing up in the Valley, I have many fond memories of the mall and even worked there as a teenager. My dad was proud when I became the number one salesperson in the nation at Wild Pair shoe store. The key to my success? I really liked the shoes!

- **Panorama City in the North Valley**

When it opened in 1955, the Panorama Mall in Panorama City was the largest major retail center in the Valley. At the time, major retailers like The Broadway, Orbach's, J. W. Robinson's, and Montgomery Ward opened stores there. And this was the first place in the valley, and among the first in the nation, to market its stores collectively as the Panorama City Shopping Center.

In the 1970s, the mall lost several key stores and the cache that went along with them. Still, the movie theater was popular, especially among teenagers. I remember going there on Christmas Day, 1982, to see *ET the Extra-Terrestrial*. Fun fact: the father of a friend of mine played the role of a doctor in ET. He was Stephen Spielberg's real doctor and had a speaking role. His one line in the movie was, "Do you think ET has the capacity to manipulate his environment?"

But my memories of the mall go way back to my early childhood. I remember shopping there with my mom and also meeting Santa and his reindeers there when I was a young child. I even have a picture of me there crying on the big man's lap.

Today, the Panorama Mall is still there, although the shops are much different than the original ones, with stores like Walmart and Curacao. In addition, the once significantly important Orbach's building is now the site of the Valley Indoor Swap Meet.

Tip #41 Other Shopping Destinations

But shopping in the Valley is not just tied to the mall. In fact, there are plenty of other places to go to find what you're looking for, including:

- **Ventura Boulevard**

True fashionistas head to Ventura Boulevard, where dozens of exclusive boutiques can be found that will make the fashion-hungry shopper drool. Try Maxine to get fully outfitted or hint for that perfect vintage piece at the many vintage and consignment clothing shops along the Boulevard. There's Blush, an all about women's clothing boutique in Encino where new shipments arrive on a weekly basis—and nothing priced more than $100. The shop offers a special Happy Hour with discounts every Thursday from 5-7 pm, as well as other events throughout the months.

You can also find home goods at stores like Voyage et Cie, a haven for those who love scented, melting wax. In addition to candles, home fragrances and bath and body products are also sold. Seasonal candle scents arrive throughout the year, which is the same story for various gift items and household goods. Or get the best of both worlds at Soto, a multi-locale boutique that offers a variety of items ranging from home goods to clothes.

You can even find beautiful flower arrangements on the Boulevard, as locals call it. So whether you're looking for an arrangement to decorate the dinner table, send to a friend, or an order for a special occasion or large-scale event, Mulberry Row provides just what you need. The shop's team will help you create an arrangement that meshes well with the moment. You can also find bath and body products, jewelry and accessories, stationery, and books there.

If music is your thing, head to Freakbeat Records. This is the Valley's neighborhood record store with an old-school vibe and racks full of new and used vinyl and CDs with a heavy focus on rock, jazz, and soul. Of course, they stock a variety of music, but their goal is to introduce you to new, underground, or smaller label artists. There are also a number of new and used DVDs for sale. If you have collectible music and paraphernalia and want a few extra bucks, try to sell your goods to the store for cash or store credit. Or, if you want to make music, head to Norman's Rare Guitars, the Valley gem where hundreds of celebrities have visited to shop for guitars, bass, and accessories. The selection includes vintage collectibles, new and used instruments, and packages for sale. The staff is knowledgeable and can answer questions for long-time players or beginners. You can also find cool clothing there.

Lazar's Luggage Superstore is for travel enthusiasts who are always on the lookout for a good deal. They house a vast supply of luggage, totes, duffel bags, accessories, and gifts. The shop is packed to the gills with goods, so go in with a focus, or you may be distracted by everything around you. Online shopping is also encouraged, although it is always nice to survey a new suitcase in person.

The Taft Charter High School Flea Market is put on by The Melrose Trading Post. There, you can find just about anything you want, from vintage and new items to wear to one-of-a-kind art, collectibles, and cool items for your home. Every Saturday from 9 am to 5 pm, Taft High School hosts this weekly flea market. Entry is just $2, and ticket sales go directly to fundraising efforts for school programs. Enjoy live music and entertainment while you shop.

- **Hollywood Hand Me Downs**

If you're a movie and television buff who enjoys shopping thrift, you're in luck. The Valley has three shops for you filled with costumes, sets, and props from What happens to all those amazing costumes, sets, and props from your favorite shows and movies.

I once got a pair of black boots worn by Alicia Silverstone in the movie *Clueless*. I loved that movie so much that I named a dog Baldwin, the word Cher Horowitz used to describe cute stores. If you want a pair of boots worn by your favorite actress, you've just got to travel to the Valley.

- **It's A Wrap**

This Burbank store is huge—we're talking 7,000 square-foot fashio and prop resale emporium. You'll discover cool props and costume of all kinds, including some from designer names like Prada, Vivienne Westwood, and Yves St. Laurent. In addition, you'll get a steal of a deal because besides being worn by starlets from all your favorite shows and movies, they're discounted by 35-95% off retail. Look for the name of the show on the price tag to learn who wore it.

- **Previously On**

Another great place to check out in Burbank is a store called Previously On. They specialize in props from your favorite show or movie and receive their product when Studios get rid of furniture and other set props. This showroom tends to carry more high-end items than the others at a fraction of what you'd have to pay if they were brand new. So go ahead and make your couch the star of your living room.

- **Western Costume Company**

This is the place to go if you're planning on winning that Halloween costume contest. Located in the heart of North Hollywood, Western Costume Company opened in 1921. And you can find true gems culled from movie sets dating back to the early days of Hollywood to binge-worthy favorites of today.

Chapter Review

- The Brady House from the popular show is located in the Valley.
- A herd of Longhorn cattle acts as ambassadors for the Leonis Adobe Monument in Calabasas.
- The author of Tarzan of the Apes lived in the Valley, and there's a museum there dedicated to his main character in the book.
- Don't miss seeing the Great Wall of Los Angeles.
- Shopping is a big deal here, from malls to boutiques to second-hand shops that sell movie memorabilia and clothes.

Chapter 3: How to Get There and Get Around

It's true, nobody walks in LA, especially when it comes to the Valley where everything you want to do is spread out. So, here are the details for planes, trains, automobiles, and more:

Tip #42 Airports

The Valley offers two convenient airports. One offers a number of direct non-stop flights. The other is for private plane owners, news helicopters along with private planes owned by the Los Angeles Fire Department, Police Department, and even helicopters for the Water and Power Department.

- **The Hollywood Burbank Airport**

I personally love this airport. The traffic alone, or lack of traffic, I should say, is enough to make me choose this airport over LAX. Plus, it's super easy to park here and much less expensive, even for the Valet. Once, I forgot to leave my keys for them, and somehow, they parked my car anyway. Just don't follow my example! The long lines you find at other airports don't exist here, but there are still a number of domestic flights, many non-stop, to get you where you need to go. I love the Jet Blue flights to and from New York. There's a direct rail connection to Downtown Los Angeles for those who don't live in the Valley. And the airport offers many domestic flights, as well as services to Canada. Keep an eye out for celebrities here who prefer the smaller crowds.

- **The Van Nuys Airport**

The Van Nuys Airport opened back in 1928. Today, you won't find service from any major airlines here. Instead, this is the spot for small planes and helicopters. Still, the airport's runways are busy, with almost 250,000 flights annually. We're talking news and tour helicopters, alongside the air operations for the Los Angeles City Fire and Police Departments, medical helicopters, and more.

'll never forget the time my then boyfriend flew me in his small personal plane from San Diego to Van Nuys on Christmas Eve. As a recent college graduate working in television news, a guy from the station offered to chauffeur me home for the holidays. I didn't realize he had a big crush on me at the time. I was clueless back then. My parents waited on the tarmac for us, big smiles on their faces. He's someone I think about even today as the one that got away. Ahh...the being young and stupid!

Tip #43 Rapid Transit

Since the Valley is so huge, various rapid transit options can be found here. However, if you plan to tour the Valley sans car, good luck. There are very few streets that cross the Valley, so if you're going the public transportation route, you'll have to plan in advance and be ready for lots of transfers.

Let's look at Valley subways first. Check with the Los Angeles County Metropolitan Transportation Authority about the Metro Line subway system, which has several stations in the Valley, namely in Universal City and North Hollywood. These lines connect to Hollywood and Downtown Los Angeles and connect the Valley with the regional Metro light rail and subway network. You can also travel Amtrak, Metrolink, Metro Rapid, Metro Local, and more. I suggest you rent a car because traveling in the Valley or anywhere in Los Angeles can be very confusing. My mind is spinning just researching this topic.

Let's turn to travel by bus. There are routes that run east to west and connect Woodland Hills with North Hollywood. From there, you can jump on a bus and travel through the Valley corridor to Pasadena.

You can also travel from the Woodland Hills bus hub north through Canoga Park to Chatsworth via the Metrolink train station and from the Woodland Hills hub north through Canoga Park to the Chatsworth via the Metrolink train station.

Still, my dad used to take the bus to work every day. It was a straight shot on Nordhoff street with the bus stop just around the corner from our house in Northridge. His job at Rockwell International was at the end of Nordhoff street, so the bus was a great way for him to get there. My mom never drove the freeway system, and anyway, they kept an old 1958 Ford with questionable brakes, so probably for the best.

Tip #44 Notable Streets and Freeways

Notable streets include:

- Sepulveda Boulevard
- Ventura Boulevard
- Laurel Canyon Boulevard
- San Fernando Road
- Victory Boulevard
- Reseda Boulevard
- Riverside Drive
- Mulholland Drive
- Topanga Canyon Boulevard.

Major freeways that cross the Valley include:

- Interstate 405, aka the San Diego Freeway
- U.S. Route 101, aka the Ventura Freeway
- The Hollywood Freeway
- State Route 118, aka the Ronald Reagan Freeway
- State Route 170, aka the Hollywood Freeway
- Interstate 210, aka the Foothill Freeway
- Interstate 5, aka Golden State Freeway.

Tip #45 Trains, Metro Rail, and Metrolink

The Metrolink commuter rail has two major Valley lines:

- The Antelope Valley Line
  Which connects the Valley to Union Station, Palmdale, and Lancaster
- The Ventura County Line
  Which connects the Valley to downtown Los Angeles

Then there's the Amtrack's Pacific Surfliner, which offers a beautiful ride along the coast. I highly recommend it. I took the Amtrack numerous times to get home from San Diego State University in my old college days. Back then, the trip was dirt cheap. And even today, it's probably less expensive than the gas it takes to get back and forth; plus, it's just such a heavenly experience. This rail line stops in the Valley at the Burbank Airport station as well as the Van Nuys and Chatsworth Stations. It travels north to Ventura County, Santa Barbara, Northern California, and south to Union Station in downtown Los Angeles and San Diego.

Tip #46 Flyaway Buses

The LAX FlyAway® bus is the best way to get to and from LAX for those who live in the Valley. This service runs seven days a week out of the Van Nuys Airport. You'll be flying past the traffic back up because the bus can use the diamond lane, aka the carpool lane. These lanes were designed to manage traffic and encourage ridesharing, but the traffic seems to get worse every year. Just wave at those angry people on the 405 waiting for the traffic to move, inch by inch. The parking is cheap too, and secure.

When leaving LAX, passengers can board buses on the Lower/Arrivals Level located in front of each terminal. Look for the blue FlyAway® columns. Just make sure to board the right bus because FlyAway buses travel to other areas. And then sit back, enjoy the ride and the free Internet access and charging stations found under the seats.

Tip #47 Taxis and Uber and Rental Cars

There are many ways to travel in and around the Valley. And for easy, stress-free transportation options, turn to taxis or ride-sourcing services like Uber.

Let's start with the taxi service. Authorized taxis include:

- Bell Cab Company
- Beverly Hills Cab Company
- City Cab
- Independent Taxi
- United Checker Cab
- United Independent Taxi Drivers (UITD)
- United Taxi of San Fernando Valley (UTSFV)
- Yellow Cab

Ride sourcing services:

Lyft, Opoli, and Uber are also authorized to work in the Valley, so be sure to download the app to your favorite service before you travel.

And all the major car rental agencies operate in the Valley, too, including:

- Avis
- Budget
- Enterprise
- Hertz
- National
- Alamo
- Turo, a car-sharing service where you can use cars from locals

Chapter Review

- The Valley is big, and while there are some transportation options, the best way to get around is by car.
- The Flyaway is your best option to and from the airport.
- If you can, use the Hollywood Burbank Airport to avoid the crowds and traffic at Los Angeles International.
- Notable streets include Sepulveda Blvd., Ventura Blvd., and Laurel Canyon.
- Freeways are the main arteries, including the 405 and the 101.

Chapter 4: Where to Stay

Stay where celebrities live, work, and play:

Tip #48 Upscale Hotels

The Valley offers a wide variety of places to stay. From fancy to family-friendly, it's all in the valley. Oh, and did I mention great meeting and event spaces too?

- **Four Seasons Westlake Village**

Set on 20 acres of exotic gardens and waterfalls, this 5-Star property offers luxury accommodations and fine dining. Home to the largest spa in the Four Seasons collection, the property boasts a relaxed yet refined California vibe. Besides a family-friendly atmosphere, this resort offers one of the most comprehensive spa and wellness programs in Los Angeles. Here, recreation, rolling hills, sandy beaches, and Southern California's best climate meet a wealth of activities, wellness, and culinary experiences to relax, reconnect, renew, and recharge.

All the property's 269 guest rooms and the 39 suites offer furnishing customized with attention to detail, like the high ceiling painted in cool colors like robin's egg, alongside botanical prints. You'll find customized Four Seasons signature beds, luxury bathrooms with granite and marble accents, large separate tubs, and my personal favorite, L'Occitane toiletries.

Besides in-room dining, guests can enjoy wood-fired meals created with local ingredients at the resort's Coin & Candor, a California Brasserie. ONYX offers a delicious menu of Nigiri sushi and sashimi made at the sushi bar, along with traditional Japanese dishes and a election of sake. The resort's Prosperous Penny offers meals to remember, and there's also poolside dining for lunch along a gourmet coffee shop called Stir.

- **The Anaz**

f you plan to bring along a four-legged family member, this is the place to go. Among the 122 rooms and suites, some are pet friendly. This boutique hotel is a great option if you enjoy the great outdoors. Located in celebrity central Calabasas, it puts you in the enviable position of being a short drive from the beach and hundreds of hiking trails. What sets The Anaz apart from other Valley hotels is its laid-back charm and small-town vibe. The Anza is also within walking distance of many excellent restaurants.

Other features include a heated pool, fitness center, complimentary Wi-Fi, and 24/7 business center. There's also a kiosk for printing airline boarding passes etc.

The Anza is the ideal place to stay if you're visiting neighboring Woodland Hills, Agoura Hills, Thousand Oaks, and the Warner Center corporate parks.

- **Airtel Plaza Hotel & Conference Center**

The Airtel Plaza Hotel is located at the Van Nuys Airport. After a long day exploring the Valley, you'll be happy to lay down on the comfy beds and luxury bedding. There are three dining options here featuring delicious cuisine made with local ingredients.

- **Beverly Garland's Holiday Inn Universal Studios**

In 1970, legendary Hollywood actress Beverly Garland, and her husband Fillmore Crank, discovered this seven-acre property. They knew they wanted to create a bucolic hideaway for friends, family, and guests. So, with the help of a Las Vegas hotel entrepreneur, they decided to build one of the most stunning hotels in North Hollywood, and they did!

Today, the property is known for being warm and welcoming yet retro, located near Universal Studios and everything else the Valley has to offer. Virtually every design detail evokes the whimsy of a bygone era. Sun pours in the floor-to-ceiling windows. This urban oasis, secluded within seven lush acres, is only minutes from Angeles.

An open fireplace warms visitors to the Front Yard, a neighborhood gathering place. Artisanal cocktails, farm-fresh eats, and a vegan menu are available. Play Uno, Taboo, or Cards Against Humanity in the courtyard.

- **Hilton Los Angeles/Universal City**

At the entrance of Universal Studios Hollywood, with wonderful views and great dining, you'll find the Hilton Los Angeles/Universal City. The recipient of the prestigious AAA Four Diamond Award as well as Green Seal Gold certification, guests may use their Hilton Honors rewards to book special packages and seasonal promotions.

This property has also received the Successful Meetings' Pinnacle Award and Smart Meetings' Platinum Award. Obviously, it's an excellent choice for meetings and events of all sizes. There's even a complimentary shuttle to and from CityWalk. The location is a short drive to Dodger Stadium and the Hollywood Bowl. The nearby Metro is just a stop away from Hollywood and Highland.

- **Marriott Burbank Airport Hotel and Convention Center**

The Los Angeles Marriott Burbank Airport welcomes guests with spacious rooms, modern amenities, and a prime Southern California location. Recharge your batteries in modern, pet-friendly hotel rooms with plush bedding, mini-refrigerators, flat-screen TVs, large work desks, and Wi-Fi. Reserve your stay in a concierge-level room with lounge access and free breakfast.

Situated near the Hollywood Burbank Airport, Universal Studios Hollywood, the North Hollywood Arts District, and Burbank Town Center, this property is extremely central to the heart of Burbank.

Delicious meals can be enjoyed at the Daily Grill, offering California cuisine and specialty cocktails. In addition, a 24-hour fitness center and an outdoor pool area are on the premises.

Choose from over 46,000 square feet of event space for meetings, weddings, and conferences.

- **Sheraton Agoura Hills Hotel**

Located along the base of the Santa Monica Mountains, Sheraton Agoura Hills Hotel offers spacious hotel rooms or suites complete with room service. This property has unparalleled access to El Matador State Beach, Pepperdine University, and Westlake Village. In addition, many breweries, trails, and wineries are just moments from its doorstep.

Fuel up for the day at Share, the hotel's restaurant with locally inspired meals. The lounge Liquid serves lighter fare and cocktails. Then, plan your corporate or social event in one of our 13 adaptable rooms featuring modern designs, high-speed Wi-Fi, and AV equipment. Whether traveling for business or pleasure, Sheraton

Agoura Hills Hotel will do everything possible to ensure a pleasant stay.

- **Sheraton Universal**

Nestled below the Hollywood Hills, the AAA 4-diamond Sheraton Universal Hotel is steps away from Universal Studios Hollywood and CityWalk. It's also a short walk to Metro's red line, where guests can easily reach the Walk of Fame, the Hollywood Bowl, and Grauman's Chinese Theatre.

The property's 451 guest rooms and 30 suites pay tribute to its Hollywood roots and offer modern ambiance as well as the Sheraton Signature Sleep Experience®. There's also free Wi-Fi, smart TV, and windows with stunning views of the Valley and Hollywood Hills.

After a complimentary breakfast, take the property's free shuttle to Universal Studios Hollywood theme park. Then, relax at the pool before finishing your day at In the Mix, the sleek hotel bar.

As far as events go, the property has an on-site executive meeting specialist to help you arrange corporate functions. With more than 30,000 square feet of meeting space – the Sheraton Universal is a memorable destination.

- **Sportsmen's Lodge Hotel**

If you're searching for the true Hollywood experience, Sportsmen's Lodge is the answer. This iconic space is more than just another Los Angeles hotel. Its legendary halls pre-date the film industry and have been graced by the likes of Katherine Hepburn and Clark Gable. Today, the property offers full-service accommodations only minutes from Valley attractions.

Featuring spacious guest rooms and suites, perks include Wi-Fi, deluxe bath amenities, and large work areas. Dine in-room, at the Patio Café, or while at the pool. Guests will soon be able to enjoy the new Sportsmen's Lodge retail space offering additional dining options and best-in-class health, beauty, and lifestyle amenities.

This is the place of memorable weddings, events, and corporate meetings. The property's singular focus is exceeding the expectations of every guest.

- **Warner Center Marriott Hotel**

The newly re-energized Warner Center Marriott Woodland Hills doesn't just offer a great night's sleep; it offers a resort-like experience. Unwind by the poolside Urban Oasis featuring lush foliage, intimate cabanas, a fire pit, and a bar.

This hotel is just a short drive from Hollywood, Los Angeles, Burbank, and Simi Valley. After visiting Malibu beaches and enjoying local attractions, find sophisticated amenities at this north LA hotel, including select rooms and suites with access to the exclusive M Club Lounge. Upscale accommodations feature plush bedding, 50-inch flat-panel HDTVs, and private balconies.

Start your day with a cup of coffee at the Starbucks café or get your heart racing in the fitness center. Later, visit the Q Martini Bar or Asado, the indoor/outdoor restaurant offering exceptional cuisine and ambiance.

- **Holiday Inn Express Hotel & Suites Woodland Hills**

This hotel is located in Woodland Hills, a five-minute drive from Westfield Promenade Shopping Mall and Westfield Topanga. It is

16 miles from Universal Studios Hollywood and about the same distance to UCLA.

The hotel's 86 air-conditioned rooms have refrigerators, microwaves, pillowtop beds, complimentary internet, flat-screen televisions, and bathrooms with shower/tub combinations. In addition, there is a pool, fitness center, and discounted use of a nearby fitness facility.

Guests enjoy a complimentary buffet breakfast daily, a 24-hour business center, and complimentary newspapers. If you're planning an event in Woodland Hills, this hotel is a good choice, with facilities measuring 624 square feet and a meeting room. Parking is free.

Tip #49 Bed & Breakfast and Air B&Bs

There are a few Bed & Breakfast gems to be found in the Valley where you will experience what it's like to be a full-time resident. Or you can also rent from residents in the Valley through Air B&B, starting at only $20 a night.

The most popular Bed & Breakfast in the Valley are:

- **Topanga Canyon Inn**

If you're seeking a rural yet cozy place to stay, it doesn't get much better than the Topanga Canyon Inn. The Mediterranean-styled Inn is tucked away on a hillside with amazing views of the Santa Monica Mountains right in the middle of Topanga State Park, yet it's close to all the fun. Topanga Canyon is known as a town filled with free spirits and everything that goes along with that vibe.

recommend you explore the canyon. It's beautiful and filled with wildlife. Plus, the Inn will take care of your every need while you're out having fun. And you'll be a short 20-minute scenic ride to Malibu. But don't worry about packing your beach essentials because the Inn will provide them for you. Just ask the front desk for some beach towels, chairs, and an umbrella before you head out. When you arrive, ask for a hiking map because you'll be staying at hike central.

As far as the breakfast goes, it's served every morning in the Casa Rosa dining room. There's also a fully stocked kitchen guests are invited to use. There are also common balconies and decks, the perfect place to meet with other guests and find out how their vacation is going.

- **Sweet Dreams Bed & Breakfast**

This is a family-oriented B&B run by a couple of empty nesters who decided to open their homes for others to enjoy. They turned the four bedrooms of the Sherman Oaks home into beautiful, reimagined suites.

Staying there puts you in the heart of things in the Valley and is just a short drive away from Hollywood and all there is to do. You'll be close to one of my favorite hiking spots, Runyan Canyon. When you get to the top, there's a little high bench that looks out over Los Angeles. Plus, you'll wake up to what former guests say is the best breakfast in Sherman Oaks!

The most unique and popular Air B&Bs include:

- **The Guest House in the Valley**

A guesthouse in Arleta is famous for being the filming location for the fictitious McFly family in the Back to the Future series. The dream of the 1950s is alive and well, thanks to the sturdy homes built during the postwar boom. With easy access to the 5, 405, and 118 freeways, Arleta is convenient to many Valley attractions. Although the neighborhood has little green space, nearby recreational facilities at Devonwood, Ritchie Valens, and Hansen Dam parks offer outdoor activities.

- **Glamping Airstream in Topanga Village**

Stay at a unique Streamline Trailer tucked into gorgeous Topanga Canyon. Amenities include a kitchenette, television, bathroom, private yard, and cozy bedroom. The village is just a five-minute walk to restaurants, shopping, and entertainment. Topanga State Park is just around the corner and features 36 miles of trails through open grassland with spectacular views of the Pacific Ocean. The largest wildland within the boundaries of a major city, this park offers recreational opportunities for hikers, mountain bikers, and equestrians. It is bordered on the south by Pacific Palisades and Brentwood, on the west by Topanga Canyon, and east by Rustic Canyon. Geologic formations such as earthquake faults, volcanic intrusions, and sedimentary formations can be found here.

- **Pet-friendly Room on an Old Farm Property.**

Private with no close neighbors or shared spaces, this 3/4-acre nursery offers a rare chance to experience rustic living in the heart of the Valley. Reflecting the rich history of Valley farms, this property dates back to 1933 when it was just a traditional chicken farm. Now a tree nursery, it remains one of the last working home farms in the Valley.

- **Artist's Cabin in Topanga**

This private cabin on gated property is located next to the wilderness, with hundreds of miles of fire roads and hiking trails. Guests enjoy skylights above a queen bed and beautiful tile mosaic, two of the many things that make this a unique retreat.

A great escape from urban life, this tiny cabin is far from the roar of civilization. Imagine yourself in another world even though you are only 22-miles from downtown Los Angeles, a 15-minute drive to the beach, or 30-minutes to Santa Monica. More than 70 oaks create a beautiful outdoor space. Guests have reportedly seen mountain lions, bobcats, foxes, and coyotes in the oldest vineyard in Topanga.

Chapter Review

- There are several upscale hotels in the Valley, like the Four Season's Westlake Village.
- You can also stay at one of several hotels near Universal Studios.
- Looking for a Bed & Breakfast? Head to Topanga Canyon Inn
- There are numerous B&B's, too, including a pet-friendly room on an old farm property with rustic charm galore.
- Or you can Glamp in an Airstream in Topanga Canyon.

Chapter 5: Arts, Culture, And Amusement

Explore the area's creativity and fun.

Tip #50 Museums

- **The Nethercutt Collection**

This museum in Sylmar is renowned for its collection of classic automobiles. More than 130 of the world's best antique, vintage, classic, and special interest cars are on display here. The collection includes top winners of the Pebble Beach Concours d'Elegance, once owned by movie stars and royalty. Visitors may see the perfectly restored 1937 Canadian Pacific Royal Hudson Locomotive #2839 built by Montreal Locomotive Works. Its royal maroon, gold leaf, glossy black, and brushed stainless steel livery pay homage to the grand era of steam locomotives. Also beautifully restored and on display is a 1912 Pullman Private Car #100 custom-built for Clara Baldwin Stocker, the daughter of pioneer "Lucky" Baldwin.

Founder J.B. Nethercutt spent a lifetime building this collection. It began in 1956 with the purchase of two automobiles. He paid $5,000 for a 1936 Duesenberg Convertible Roadster and $500 for a 1930 DuPont Town Car; both cars needed total refurbishing. JB meticulously rebuilt them and won the coveted Best of Show award at the prestigious Pebble Beach Concours d'Elegance. By 1992, his cars had won the Pebble Beach Concours d'Elegance six times, more than any other individual.

As JB's collection grew in size, he was determined to share it with the public. So he and Dorothy opened a magnificent museum in the foothills of the San Gabriel Mountains in 1971. Admission is free.

- **Valley Relics Museum**

This Museum in Van Nuys is devoted to history and pop culture. Its collection is so large that it occupies two airport hangers in an industrial park adjacent to Van Nuys Airport. Both aviation and the entertainment industry are reflected in the museum's displays. Relics from B-Westerns and classic cars are presented alongside restaurant memorabilia, BMX bikes, pinball machines, neon signs, and more. Valley Relics Museum is a great education in suburban history. The non-profit is the brainchild of Valley native Tommy Gelinas.

"I took it upon myself to try and seek out my history and figure out what happened to all these wonderful establishments. Pieces of architecture and places I used to hang out, realizing they're gone forever," says Gelinas. So in 2015, his collection outgrew his garage, and he established the first Valley Relics Museum in a Chatsworth warehouse. He moved the museum to its current home five years later, which displays more than 25,000 items.

In addition to Gelinas' personal items, the community has made many contributions, including Roddy McDowall's chimp mask from Planet of the Apes, a Hires root beer collection, a bedroom door from The Brady Bunch donated by actress Eve Plumb, Charlie Chaplin's pajamas, Mike Connor's suit from Mannix, and more.

- **Gordon R. Howard Museum complex in Burbank**

What began as a search about her father's years as Burbank's police chief became an obsession for Mary Jane Strickland. She discovered inaccuracies in the city's records and inquired about methods for preservation. The city library was already storing many historical documents and photographs, but Strickland decided more had to be done. She founded the Burbank Historical Society in 1973 and was quoted as saying, "I just started collecting things, putting things together and talking to people, and pretty soon I was a woman possessed."

Did you know that the first monorail patented in the US was actually designed and built in Burbank? Burbank was also once home to many wineries. Early farmers found the soil ideal for growing grapes. Learn many interesting facts when visiting this museum complex.

- **The Museum of the San Fernando Valley in Northridge**

The Museum began in 2005 in a historic bungalow located on the campus of LA. Valley College. Small grants provided the necessary funding to create exhibits and events for the next three years. The Museum eventually moved to the Fashion Square Mall in Sherman Oaks, where thousands of people visited each month. Today the city of Northridge is the museum's home in the western San Fernando Valley. The collection includes interactive exhibits, lectures, performances, and visits for schools and organizations interested in learning more about the San Fernando Valley.

Tip #51 Universal Studios and the Universal Studios CityWalk

It's no wonder that Universal Studios Hollywood™ is called the Entertainment Capital of LA. Your visit requires at least a full day to explore the movie-based theme park, take the Studio Tour and have un at Universal CityWalk®. There is also entertainment, shopping, nd dining options, including Universal Cinema and the "5 'owers," the state-of-the-art concert venue. In addition, Universal tudios Hollywood features real-life interpretations of iconic novies and television shows from The Wizarding World of Harry 'otter™ to King Kong 360 3-D and a fully immersive Skull Island.

ntrance here also includes rides on Harry Potter and the 'orbidden Journey™ and Flight of the Hippogriff™, Universal tudios Hollywood's first outdoor rollercoaster.

very summer during my college years, I worked in food service at he park. The job paid very well and was so much fun because most f the people who worked there were my age. One day, I was sent to he front of the park with a lemonade cart when suddenly, I heard unshots. Two men with guns ran past me, and I immediately hid under my cart. People waiting in line to enter the park began lapping. Apparently, they thought it was part of the tour!

also met the employee who wore the Frankenstein costume. He old me about a parakeet he needed to rehome. The bird's name was ammy Davis, Jr. When he told me that Sammy was missing an eye, was sold. He lived to a ripe old age and always flew sideways due o his missing eye!

)ther immersive attractions include Despicable Me Minion Jayhem, Super Silly Fun Land, and the Springfield, the hometown f America's favorite TV family, adjacent to the award-winning The impson's Ride.

s far as the Studio Tour goes, guests can go behind the scenes of he world's busiest movie and television studio and experience thrill ides like Fast & Furious—Supercharged.

Universal CityWalk is a Southern California entertainment destination with acres of fun in an environment that reflects the area's cultural diversity. Try traditional Mexican favorites like fajitas, tacos, or enchiladas at Antojitos Cocina Mexicana. The open-air complex provides many entertainment options; the dynamic high-tech concert venue, "5 Towers," LA's best movie-going experience at Universal Cinema, with a 7-story IMAX®, LASER theatre, and iFly indoor skydiving.

Tip #52 Warner Brothers Studios and Tour

Believe it or not, Warner Brothers Studio originated with a gamble taken by four brothers who believed audiences would like 'talkies'— motion pictures syncing speech and sound.

As with most innovations, early attempts failed. But in 1927, Warner Bros. released The Jazz Singer and changed the silver screen forever. Today, Warner Brothers is in the heart of Burbank, where it remains a working studio. While on Warner Bros. Studio Tour Hollywood, guests can get a birds-eye view of sets and sound stages where that tradition lives on. From Casablanca to The Music Man, Friends to ER, Ellen to Conan—this is where guests get to see what happens behind the scenes.

According to the Warner Brothers website: "The tours focus on how production happens ... and that will inspire people to not only understand what goes on in the making of a film but to experiment themselves. Most people have no clue what is involved. But the tour can be a tool for people to learn and really express themselves."

After graduating from college, I got a job at Warner Brothers working as a tour guide. I enjoyed meeting many celebrities backstage at The Tonight Show. My all-time favorite was Jimmy tewart. He was, of course, tall but also extremely nice and had uch a beautiful, distinctive voice. Yes, I was living a wonderful life ack then!

Tip #53 North Hollywood Arts District

The NoHo Arts District is a one-square-mile community in North Hollywood. It is home to more than 20 live, professional theatres, dance studios, art galleries, music recording venues, acting and art workshops, international dining options, specialty shops, and businesses. NoHo is "Where the Arts Are Made." Live music and other performance make it an absolute paradise of self-expression.

Tip #54 Valley Performing Arts Center

The Valley Performing Arts Center is located on the campus of California State University, Northridge, on Nordhoff Street. The Center provides an alternative arts venue to downtown Los Angeles. Framed around a spectacular glass lobby, it consists of a 1,700-seat hall, educational spaces for the Theater Department, a large lecture hall, and a studio for the university's radio station KCSN-FM. The Center's award-winning architecture draws many fans.

Performances are selected to appeal to all of LA's richly diverse communities. Each season includes a vibrant performance schedule of nearly 50 classical and popular music, dance, theater, family, and international events putting the Center at the cultural and intellectual heart of the San Fernando Valley.

Tip #55 The San Fernando Valley Arts & Cultural Center

The mission of SFVCACC is to advocate art and culture through education and philanthropy. Virtual exhibitions, global outreach, and online courses highlight local, national, and international artists. Since 2015, its Southern California Regional Exhibitions (SCORE) project has promoted many art disciplines. The SFVACC also partners with artist Co-op 7 and offers Zoom-based art course: workshops, and lectures. Art courses have attracted participants from as far away as Canada and Guatemala.

Tip #56 Mural Mile

You will find many beautiful murals along three miles of Van Nuys Boulevard surrounding Pacoima City Hall. Pacoima native Levi Ponce and his collaborators created more than a dozen of the 50 murals along the Mural Mile. Their work depicts important Latino figures ranging from Frida Kahlo and Salvador Dali to Diego River; and actor Danny Trejo.

Tip #57 The Starlight Bowl

The Starlight Bowl in Burbank is a 5,000-seat amphitheater for concerts, performances, and school events. Constructed in 1950, it seats 3,000 in chairs and 2,000 more on the lawn. Overlooking the San Fernando Valley and Los Angeles, the Starlight Bowl is open to the public every summer. One of the annual highlights is the 4th of July show. The 2021 celebration starred the Tonight Show All-Star Band with guest vocalist Gloria Loring followed by a spectacular fireworks display.

Tip #58 Busch Gardens

The San Fernando Valley was formerly home to an amusement par: in Van Nuys. Busch Gardens, located at the Budweiser Brewery mid-Valley, had a single theme, naturally beer!

The tropical, family, fun-oriented Busch Gardens was hugely popular from 1966 to 1979. Busch began when Adolphus Busch, who worked in the brewery supply business in St. Louis, married the daughter of struggling brewery operator Eberhard Anheuser in 1861. When Anheuser died in the 1880s, the company re-emerged as Anheuser-Busch, manufacturing Budweiser in St. Louis while ling to go national.

According to biographers, Busch lived an extravagant lifestyle with palatial homes all over the country. One Pasadena home was surrounded by lush gardens, open to the public from 1905 to 1937, and later became known as the first Busch Gardens.

It wasn't until 1966 that Busch Gardens, Van Nuys, opened. At its peak, the tourist attraction was home to a bird show, boat rides, free Budweiser, Michelob, Busch Bavarian beer, and a monorail tour of the entire facility that smelled like yeast. Unfortunately, this attraction was demolished in the 1970s to make room for expansion.

With Busch Gardens no longer in existence, the only amusement park in the Valley is Universal Studios Hollywood in unincorporated Universal City. More movies and television shows are filmed here than in any other lot in the world.

Chapter Review

- Don't miss the Universal Studios Tour, a full day of backlot fun.
- Another not to miss tour is of the Warner Brothers Studio.
- See tributes to important Latino figures like Frida Kahlo and Salvador Dali at the Mural Mile.
- In the summer, head to the Starlight Bowl for some music and fun under the stars.

- Don't miss the NoHo Arts District's art galleries and dining options.

Chapter 6: Drinking, Dining, And Clubbing

No matter what your preference, any type of food can be found in the Valley.

Tip #59 Jewish Delis

Jewish delis are one of the highlights of the Valley's dining scene. In addition to these casual stalwarts, there is an emerging breed of contemporary delicatessens offering modern twists while still staying true to traditional flavors. The area's most famous delis include:

- **Brent's Delicatessen in Northridge**

Brent's Deli is an institution in the Valley with a menu of timeless food. Considered to be one of the best places for pastrami in the greater LA area, Brent's also serves a grilled, black forest pastrami Reuben. Its strip mall location is reminiscent of the 1970s, and everything from the matzo ball soup to the deli meats is worth the visit.

- **Art's Delicatessen and Restaurant**

This is another Valley institution where every sandwich is a masterpiece. Located on Ventura Boulevard in Sherman Oaks, Art's Deli has been a popular spot since its opening in 1957. The Northridge earthquake inflicted heavy damage in 1994, and the original owner Art Ginsburg has since died, but the deli is still there and still famous for its blintzes, corned beef, and other classics.

Tip #60 Asian Influence

The main thoroughfare of the San Fernando Valley is Ventura Boulevard stretching from Studio City to Calabasas. A portion of it is also known as Sushi Row for the sheer number of Japanese restaurants. Here are some local favorites:

- **Asanebo**

The recipient of a Michelin star back in 2009, this restaurant has an impressive selection of hot, fusion dishes on its menu that are as good as the sushi. Foodies swear by the seared toro. Tarzana's Sushi Spot is known for its expansive a la carte selection. Dinner starts at $37 and lunch combos start at $10. We recommend the raw octopus and uni a la carte.

- **Okumura**

This restaurant is lauded for its highly skilled chefs and sushi roll specialists. In addition to a large selection of sushi and sashimi, the sauces are homemade with secret ingredients that cannot be replicated anywhere else.

- **Sugarfish**

Only the traditional sushi of the highest quality based on Chef Nozawa's recipe is served omakase-style. Choose from three options. Locals recommend "Surprise Me." My friend Brenda drives for miles from her home near Six Flags Magic Mountain to eat at Sugarfish. And Brenda is a true foodie!

Tip #61 Food from Around the World

But, when it comes to delicious food, there's a lot more to the 818 than yellowtail and omakase.

- **Gorilla Pies**

This restaurant serves Pittsburgh-style pizza with California soul. The dough is a hybrid using both natural fermentation and commercial yeast at 65% hydration. Only the best gourmet flour from Caputo and King Arthur is used, along with organic Bianco di Napoli tomatoes.

- **Gasolina Café**

Some of LA's best Spanish food may be found in Woodland Hills. That's where Gasolina Cafe owner Sandra Cordero creates dishes like pan tomate, tortilla española, and weekend paellas.

- **Apey Kade Restaurant**

The tremendous range of Sri Lankan food is on full display in Tarzana. You'll find it all on the menu, from raw kale salads to hearty soups and stews.

- **Vinh Loi Tofu**

Reseda's Vinh Loi Tofu is a hit with herbivores and omnivores alike. Its extensive menu of Vietnamese classics is prepared without animal protein. Any dish containing the restaurant's signature made-from-scratch tofu is sure to please.

- **Lum-Ka Naad**

Valley dwellers don't have to make the trip to Thai Town to find extraordinary Thai fare. Lum-Ka Naad is the go-to destination if you have been craving spicy northern and southern Thai specialties However, locals say to order with caution.

- **Tel Aviv Glatt Koser Grill**

Local foodies will say this Kosher micro-chain makes some of LA's best Israeli food. Sabich, schnitzel, challah, and shawarma anyone?

- **Furnsaj Bakery**

This Granada Hills bakery serves some of the best Lebanese food in Los Angeles. According to patrons, shawarma is a must-order, and the flatbreads are heavenly.

- **Mizlala**

Refined Mediterranean fare in Sherman Oaks? Absolutely! And it serves an exciting menu of small plates and tagines that are worth the drive over the hill. Petit Trois. Offering an extensive menu of French bistro fare, Petit Trois in Sherman Oaks is open for both outdoor and indoor dining and serves everything from the perfect omelet to the Big Mec. Be sure to try the house-made bread. Yum!

- **Boneyard Bistro**

This famed barbecue joint in Sherman Oaks continues to turn out quality, slow-cooked meats and sides. Locals can't decide which to order. The ribs? Brisket? Or one of the deviled eggs? Oh, and did we mention beer? There's that too.

- **Portos Bakery & Café**

This family-run business offers an array of delicious options. Thankfully, there are several locations in and around the Valley. When you buy a delicious pastry, you can feel good about eating it because the chain supports Children's Hospital. Plus, they even offer some goodies you can bake at home. Cheese roll, anyone?

Tip #62 Italian

Something special about the Valley's Italian restaurants makes guests want to come back for more. Could it be the ambiance? The scent? The fresh ingredients? The flavor? How about all three, especially when exploring the restaurants listed below.

- **Pasta Bar**

This Michelin Guide Pasta Bar is tucked away in an Encino strip mall, but don't let the location fool you. This local hot spot offers refined Italian dishes. An industrial space with cement floors and funky lighting sets the tone. Regulars recommend the tasting menu.

- **Pinocchio Restaurant and Monte Carlo Deli**

Italian food lover's dream about Burbank's Pinocchio Restaurant and Monte Carlo Deli. Eggplant parmesan, vegetable lasagna, baked ziti. Inexpensive noodles served with red sauce, meat sauce, and alfredo. You name it, and they've got it. Locals rave about the garlic bread.

Tip #63 Sandwich and Hot Dog Joints

- **Dan's Super Subs**

My brother says that if you hang out at Dan's Super Subs in Woodland Hills long enough, you'll see just about every resident of the Valley. This is because the sandwiches here are that good. Dan's Super Subs is voted the best sandwich shop in the Valley year after year.

- **Bill's Burgers**

There are burgers and burger-makers, and then there's Bill Elwell. The namesake behind this Van Nuys beef and bun legend still mans the grill as often as possible, turning out some of the heartiest and least expensive meals in the Valley. Fans love the old-school style burger for its hefty size and recommend you order one fully loaded.

- **Larry's Chili Dog**

Los Angeles is a breakfast burrito town, and there is no shortage of options in the Valley. One of the biggest contenders for the throne is Larry's Chili Dog, an old-fashioned hot dog spot for eggs and meat wrapped in tortillas. Don't miss the classic dogs with your choice of toppings.

- **Cupids Hotdogs**

There are several places around the Valley where you'll find a Cupid's Hot Dog stand. This longtime, family-run hot dog joint offers classic toppings such as chili, onions & relish. Their chili is the bomb! Before my dad had major surgery which could have cost this life, he asked for a Cupids hotdog!

- **Bill & Hirokos**

A tiny burger with big taste! Burgers here are straightforward: thin patties tucked between soft, grilled buns along with tomato, lettuce, and optional onions, grilled or raw. No secret sauce, just good 'ol mayo! It adds up to a satisfying burger that attracts legions of loyal ans who warn don't show up on Saturdays unless you're willing to wait a long time!

- **Hero Submarine Sandwich Shoppe**

Do yourself a favor and try one of these sandwiches. This unsung strip-mall gem serves vintage California-style heroes like no one else. Sandwiches are made on lightly steamed bread filled with your choice of meat and topped with their famous tomato salad. Since my early years, having a My Hero sandwich was a special treat.

Tip #64 Mediterranean

Mediterranean food in the Valley is not only delicious, it's healthy. That's because the Mediterranean diet emphasizes lots of fresh whole foods such as vegetables, fruits, nuts, seeds, and legumes.

- **Mizlala**

Refined Mediterranean fare in Sherman Oaks? Absolutely! Mizlala serves an exciting menu of small plates and tagines worth the drive over the hill.

- **Esso Bistro**

Known for serving authentic Mediterranean food, Esso Bistro in Encino features comfort food grounded in Syrian and Armenian traditions. Interesting tidbit: the name refers to the childhood nickname of the owner's wife. Don't miss their creamy hummus dressed with Aleppo pepper, parsley, and olive oil.

- **Sako's Mediterranean Cuisine**

This restaurant has been specializing in Turkish and Armenian dishes since 2002. Insider tip: the Iskandar Kebab will make you feel like you've left the Valley for Turkey.

Tip #65 Fine Dining

Some of the best fine dining in Southern California can be found in the Valley. If you'd like to get dressed up and enjoy a fabulous meal you'll find lots of options in the Valley. Did we mention the views?

- **Vitello's**

Inspired by contemporary Italian cuisine, the chef-driven kitchen at Vitello's in Sherman Oaks produces classics such as piccata, marsala, and parmigiana, plus many modern dishes. Insiders tip: try the Weekend Jazz Brunch.

- **The Odyssey**

Featuring farm-to-table menus with fresh ingredients and an emphasis on skilled suppliers, the Odyssey in Granada Hills serves contemporary cuisine, quality steaks aged to perfection, and fresh seafood.

Don't miss the Sunday brunch if you're a fan of buffet dining. With distinctly elegant spaces, the Odyssey is also an exclusive and unforgettable event location with striking views of the San Fernando Valley. My Goddaughter had her sweet sixteen birthday party here, and it was so much fun! She looked just as beautiful as the view from the terrace.

- **Inn of the Seventh Ray**

ocals praise the Californian cuisine, made with seasonal, organic ngredients, served at this one-of-a-kind restaurant in Topanga Canyon. Majestic sycamores line the picturesque property, and you an dine under the stars by candlelight as you listen to gentle vaterfalls along winding pathways.

Meals prepared with great culinary finesse are charged with the ibration of the violet flame of the Seventh Ray. Is it the food or the voodland setting that makes this place so enchanting? Fans say it's little of both. I say don't miss it!

Tip #66 Best Mexican Food

The Great Debate: Is LA Mexican food better than NYC's? These ocal favorites prove the best Mexican dishes can be found in the Valley.

- **Casa Vega**

Casa Vega's charm has withstood the test of time. The casual Mexican American restaurant known for its roomy, red booths and colorful atmosphere has become a mainstay for the San Fernando Valley. It frequently acts as a backdrop for movies and TV shows. Tortilla chips and margaritas are enjoyable with big groups of riends, but sometimes sitting at the bar and chatting with the ageless staff is just as much of a treat.

- **Cilantro Mexican Grill**

North Hollywood's Cilantro Mexican Grill makes what may be the best meat burrito in the city. Found in the corner of a busy gas station, this place draws dozens of lunchtime diners eager to enjoy he food prepared by chef Adolfo Perez. He is a Le Cordon Bleu graduate and former corporate chef who is now making his dream come true.

- **The Sagebrush Cantina**

The Sagebrush Cantina was originally a group of small stores built by Lester Agoure, Sr., in the 1920s. The parking lot was a local jail, and a famous hanging tree still stands outside. Believe it or not, the tree is still the identifying logo of the Calabasas Chamber of Commerce. Today great food, awesome drinks, and live entertainment keep people coming back for more.

- **Tacos Chave**

Located in North Hollywood next to the Bank of America, where a notorious shootout took place in 1997, Tacos Chave bills itself as the best tacos "*al Estilo Puebla.*" Regulars recommend the Asada Taco. This taqueria serves the spiciest of salsas, and the salsa rojella is muy deliciouso.

Tip #67 Nightlife

Although the Valley will never live up to the beacon of LA nightlife found over the hill, it does have its fair share of unique places to go after dark.

- **Idle Hour Bar**

Who doesn't like drinking inside a two-story wooden barrel? Someone wisely bought this 90-year-old icon and turned it into a destination bar. It caters to a laid-back crowd not found in other parts of the Valley. Idle Hour Bar serves craft beer and solid cocktails and has one of the best patios in the city.

- **Tony's Darts Away**

Once you get to Tony's, you may not want to leave. The atmosphere is fun but low-key, the bar food is delicious, and the wait staff will treat you like a regular. It's also a favorite sports bar for vegans and vegetarians.

- **Tiki No**

Did you know that tiki bars originated in Los Angeles? That means that you'll find the best places to down flaming rum drinks in the country, if not the world. Tiki No is an absolute dive bar in North Hollywood, serving up a great atmosphere, fantastic cocktails, and rum punch bowls for those brave enough to try them.

- **The Red Door**

This Toluca Lake favorite is a speakeasy. A tiny red door (get it?) hidden in a mall alleyway leads to one of the Valley's best-kept secrets. With red booths and silent movies, the vibe at The Red Door is more subdued than rowdy. The food is good, too!

- **The Baked Potato Jazz Club**

This world-famous club has been home to jazz's best musicians since 1970. Stellar music and great food are available nightly. This rustic, pint-sized place is LA's oldest Jazz Club with a menu that includes baked potatoes of every description. Yummy! Plus, the live music is awesome!

Chapter Review

- Take your pick of delicious sushi restaurants on Sushi Row.

- Every sandwich is a work of art at Art's Delicatessen.
- Head to the Inn at the Seventh Ray in Topanga Canyon for delicious food and good vibes.
- Cupid's Hot Dogs serve the best chili dogs on the planet!
- Jazz anyone? Head to the Baked Potato Jazz Club.

Chapter 7: Things to Do Outside

The Valley's subtropical weather means mild, rainy winters and hot, sunny summers, perfect for great outdoors lovers.

Tip #68 Hiking Trails

Time to hit the trail in the San Fernando Valley. Hikers can find many steep slopes and breathtaking vistas in the Simi Hills, Santa Monica Mountains, Los Padres National Forest, and Angeles National Forest-San Gabriel Mountains National Monument. Here are some favorites:

- **Stough Canyon**

Come Spring, it's only a short hike into this Burbank canyon to see wildflowers and scenic overlooks. The Old Youth Campground Trail is a popular single-track trail that will loop back to your car. Remnants of an old Boy Scout camp are a popular site. On a clear day, you can see the whole city. The Stough Canyon Nature Center offers docent-led hikes for birdwatching and wildlife viewing.

- **Stoney Point Park**

In Chatsworth, right off Topanga Canyon Boulevard, you'll find a giant boulder outcropping called Stoney Point after exiting the 118 Freeway. This confluence of boulders has formed caves, dens, and alcoves perfect for climbing and exploring. Some unusual rock formations bear markings from native tribes, in this case, the Gabrielino-Tongva tribe. Hiking and bridle trails take you around the rocks, though most people prefer to climb them. This park provides a good view for trainspotters of the tracks passing through tunnel cut out of rock. Stoney Point is a mile marker for the

Southern Pacific Railroad and was originally part of the larger Transcontinental Railroad, which, unfortunately, never ended up connecting the entire country. The train's route marks the division between the Simi Hills and the Santa Susana Mountains, between Los Angeles and Ventura counties.

- **O'Melveny Park**

O'Melveny Park in Granada Hills is easy to get lost in without a map. There are a few ways to get to Mission Point, but you can't go wrong hopping onto any trail, including the equestrian trail. Visitors to the Santa Susana Mountains suggest you use the sight of the Los Angeles Reservoir to stay oriented. And don't worry, you'll find your way back as long as you head downward. Just make sure you're descending an actual trail and not a firebreak.

Tip #69 Mountain Biking

The sport of mountain biking comes with its own culture, which includes slang. So, before you take off on any of the Valley's bike trails, read up on how to sound cool when you take that booter (a large jump that requires a lot of commitment.)

- **Dirt Mulholland**

Found on the unpaved segment of the storied Mulholland Drive, Dirt Muholland is eight miles long and runs from the 101 west across the Santa Monica Mountains ending at the Pacific Coast Highway near Leo Carrillo State Park. Constructed in the 1920s to show off real estate in the San Fernando Valley and the Hollywood Hills, the trail offers unsurpassed views of the Encino Reservoir, th mountains surrounding the Valley, Los Angeles, and the Pacific. The Towsley Canyon Loop Trail. This up-and-down loop in San Fernando will get your heart pumping. Avoid weekends when it's packed with hikers. Weekdays are much more biker friendly. Regulars suggest riding the loop counterclockwise to avoid steep climbs. This technical ride has many switchbacks, so it could be difficult for beginners.

- **Cheeseboro Loop**

Much of the Agoura trail system is on fire roads, but not this ride, part of the remote Sheep Corral Trail. The trails aren't super-technical. Be advised that there's no cell service, and you'll likely be the only one out, especially on weekdays. The five-mile climb on the Palo Comado Canyon Trail leads to flatter riding, and there's a shortcut to the 12.5-mile loop via the Cheeseboro Canyon Trail.

Tip #70 Cycling

There's nothing like getting out on your bike. And in the Valley, there are many places to do just that. Here are a few examples:

- **Lake Balboa/Anthony C. Beilenson Park**

Located at 6300 Balboa Boulevard in Van Nuys, Lake Balboa is a breathtaking parkland complete with bike trails, lakes, tennis courts, and golf courses. The park is family-friendly and activity-loaded—play outdoor games, scooter, or bike on verdant lawns and winding pathways. Free parking is available around the park.

- **Serrania Park**

Located at 20726 Wells Drive, Serrania Park has a concrete sidewalk ideal for biking. Hidden in suburban Woodland Hills at Serrania Avenue and Wells Drive, Serrania Park is an outdoor lover's dream. This park offers lots of room for dogs and people to roam and includes benches, picnic tables, and a playground.

- **Lake Calabasas**

Situated at 23401 Park Sorrento in Calabasas, enjoy a bike ride amidst the spectacular scenery on a sidewalk designed explicitly for cyclists. From here, you can take a leisurely ride to Lake Calabasas Park. If you prefer Mother Nature and wildlife, there are plenty of turtles, ducks, geese, and cranes that call Lake Calabasas home.

- **Limeklin Canyon Trail**

This 3.8-mile trail near Porter Ranch starts at Rinaldi Street between Tampa Avenue and Corbin Avenue. Limekiln Canyon Trail's bike paths have some forks and a mix of paved and dirt roads offering single track and short climbs. Heads up! You'll find wild rabbits and a variety of birds as you cross a creek. Enjoy the climb to touch Tampa Avenue before descending back into the canyon. This gentle trail is not to be missed by any outdoors lover.

Tip #71 Ahmanson Ranch

Simi Valley's upper Las Virgenes Open Space Preserve, previously known as Ahmanson Ranch, was a controversial piece of land for many years. In 1989, the proposed construction of more than 3,000 homes, a golf course, and a shopping center upset residents who worried about congestion on the 101 freeway and Valley Circle Rd. Mountain lions, badgers, and other endangered species living in the corridor between the Santa Monica Mountains and Santa Susana were threatened.

In 2004, the state bought the land from Washington Mutual Bank, and today, the Las Virgenes Open Space Preserve is a park for animals and humans. There are many trails for hiking, riding, and equestrians on well-maintained fire roads, making it an excellent area for novice riders.

The Chumash Native American tribe lived on this land for centuries. Before European involvement, at least one village, Huwam, was where Chumash, Tongva, and Tataviam peoples lived. In addition, there's a cave on the land known as The Cave of Munits. A mythical shaman was killed after murdering the son of a Chumash chief.

The Victory Trailhead, located in West Hills, is the main trailhead for the Preserve. Just west of Calabasas is The Las Virgenes Canyon Road Trailhead.

Tip #72 The Japanese Gardens

An unexpected oasis lies in the middle of the San Fernando Valley, an authentic Japanese Strolling Garden. This six-and-a-half-acre paradise has three gardens: a dry Zen meditation garden, a "wet-strolling" garden, and a tea garden.

The design of the strolling garden enables the viewer to walk from one point to another while enjoying vistas from various vantage points. The dry Zen meditation garden (karesensui) contains Tortoise Island, a three-Buddha arrangement of stones, and a wisteria arbor at the end of Plover Path. The expansive Chisen or "wet-strolling" garden contains waterfalls, lakes and streams, lush greenery, and stone lanterns hand-carved by Japanese artisans. The Shoin Building, with an authentic teahouse and tea garden, sits at the end of the path. Azaleas, cherry trees, magnolias, wisteria, raphiolepis indica, iris, and lotus provide the perfect backdrop for private and public events. This authentic Japanese garden was designed by Dr. Koichi Kawana. He created more than a dozen major Japanese gardens in the United States.

Tip #73 Cherry Blossom Festival

Each Spring, a few Southern California cities celebrate their Japanese roots as delicate pink flowers begin to blossom along streets and in parks. For example, Lake Balboa Park, a popular picnic spot, springs to life when more than 2,000 cherry trees bloom around the lake's perimeter, usually in March or April. Peak blooms are short-lived, and trees tend to bloom at different times. No worries. If you miss the cherry blossoms, you can always take the swan boats for a spin.

Tip #74 Valley Greek Festival

The Valley's annual Greek Festival takes place on Memorial Day Weekend at Saint Nicholas Greek Orthodox Church. The festival highlights the simple pleasures of Greek life, celebrating the food, dance, music, and more.

Festivalgoers enjoy the distinctive sounds of the bouzouki and other exotic instruments played by Greek musicians in traditional costumes. Learn intricate dances and try delicious Greek food like gyros, pistachio, baklava, and kadaifi. Want to learn more about Greek culture and icons? A tour of the Greek Orthodox Church is also available.

Tip #75 Golf Courses

There are eleven golf courses in the Valley.

- Angeles National Golf Club is an 18-hole public course that Jack Nicklaus designed in 2004.
- Balboa Course at Sepulveda Golf Complex is a 36-hole course designed in 1953.

- Cascades Golf Club features an 18-hole course designed by Bob Cupp in 1999.
- Designed by Ted Robinson in 1963, East Course at Braemar Country Club has 36-holes.
- Van Nuys Golf Course offers a 27-hole public course designed by Joe Novak.
- El Caballero Country Club is a private, 18-hole course designed by Robert Trent Jones, Sr., in 1957.
- Robert Muir Graves designed The El Cariso Golf Course in 1977. It has 18-holes.
- Hansen Dam Golf Course has 18-holes and was established and built in 1963.
- Porter Valley Country Club is a private, 18-hole course designed by Ted Robinson and built in 1968.
- Studio City Golf Course is a 9-hole course.
- Woodley Lakes Golf Course features 18-holes designed by Ray Goates in 1965.

ip #76 The Hansen Dam

he Hansen Dam was built in 1940 in the northeastern part of the alley's Lake View Terrace neighborhood, designed to provide ecessary flood control in the Valley. Besides being a critical piece f infrastructure, it's also a recreational area.

nd recreational it is with a golf course, an equestrian center, and n aquatic area. Take the walking path around the dam or fish in he lake. It's open year-round but may be closed during events or ad weather. There's also a smaller lake that is filtered and hlorinated, perfect for swimming.

uilt in 2014, The Discovery Cube Los Angeles is at the northwest orner of the recreation area. Believe it or not, the local Sanitation ureau has created exhibits, yes, we're talking sanitation exhibits, ut these are designed to teach visitors about reducing waste and sustainability. It just sounds weird that the Bureau of Sanitation ha created exhibits, doesn't it?

Tip #77 The San Fernando Valley Film Tour

Are you a movie location buff? If the answer is "yes," then conside a bus tour. Filming locations explorer, Jared Cowan, can guide you through the Valley in a comfortable limo bus to nearly 40 iconic an hidden filming locations from your favorite movies. The three-hou tour departs from the new home of the Valley Relics Museum, which displays amazing artifacts from the historic San Fernando Valley. Tickets are available online.

Jared Cowan is a photographer and film journalist who has writter extensively on filming locations for various publications, including Los Angeles Magazine, LA TACO, and LA Weekly. His podcast, On Location with Jared Cowan, is based on interviews with filmmaker on movie locations. Find him on iTunes, Google Play Music, and SoundCloud.

Tip #78 Movies on the Roof

You're invited to take a seat atop Westfield Fashion Square's parking garage for the annual alfresco holiday film series. Each Friday and Saturday of December until Christmas, a different flick is presented, from Elf to Bad Santa to Batman Returns. Tickets support Valley-based non-profits.

Westfield Fashion Square is a shopping mall in the Sherman Oaks and Van Nuys area of Los Angeles. Its anchor stores are Bloomingdale's and Macy's. The mall originally opened in 1962 as Bullock's Fashion Square, formerly anchored by Bullock's and I. Magnin. Movies on the Roof is just one of many events it sponsors.

Chapter Review

- Witness 2,000 Cherry trees blossom at Balboa Park each Spring.
- The Japanese Garden is truly a hidden oasis.
- Tee off at any of the eleven golf courses in the Valley.
- Take the San Fernando Valley film tour to see the locations of your favorite movies and television shows.
- Movies on the Roof, anyone? Head to Westfield Fashion Square in Sherman Oaks over the Christmas holidays.
- Awesome hiking and biking trails too!

Chapter 8: Things to Do Inside

When the weather's not cooperating with your plans, there's still plenty to do indoors. Here's a rundown.

Tip #79 Day Spas

What better way to get out of the heat than visiting a day spa? Here are some good ones:

- **Burke Williams Urban Day Spa**

There are two Valley locations for this popular day spa. One is in Woodland Hills, and the other at the Sherman Oaks Galleria. I've been to the one at the Galleria, and it is a truly relaxing space. Being there is like being in a safe sanctuary. The facilities are spotless, and the technicians are very talented. Try a hot stone massage, a sports massage, or any of their facials. It's the perfect oasis to get away from the world and relax.

- **Le Rêve Salon and Spa**

Pamper yourself at this local favorite located in Granada Hills. Get your hair done by professionals, have a mani/pedi, or try any of their spa treatments. Or, for a real treat, schedule a full day there and leave looking and feeling your best.

- **Organic Spa**

Locals say the Organic Spa is the best in the area. No wonder, it's the first one to incorporate an organic concept in its Asian/Moroccan-designed eco-friendly space. Besides the usual massage and facial treatments, you can also pick up organic products to use at home.

Tip #80 Sky Zone Trampoline Park

Did you know that bouncing is good for your body and your brain? Van Nuys Sky Zone is just the place to indulge and jump to your heart's content. The originator of wall-to-wall aerial action offers annual passes, event space, and more. Sky Zone is part of CircusTrix, the world's largest developer and operator of trampoline and entertainment parks with more than 300 locations globally.

Tip #81 K1-Speed – Indoor Go-Karts

What makes K1 Speed Burbank unique? The indoor location allows individuals to race every day of the year, regardless of the weather. Old-fashioned, gas-powered go-karts have been replaced by high-performance machines, producing tremendous torque and horsepower from advanced electric motors. New electric karts are also better for the environment, quieter, and easier to handle. Stalling is no longer a worry. Speeds can reach 45 mph on the indoor track. In addition, special events and corporate packages are available.

Tip #82 The Canyon Agoura Hills

This music venue is known for old-school favorites like Buddy Guy, Taj Mahal, Foghat, The Tubes, The Motels, Billy Bob Thornton, and the Boxmasters. This intimate, 610-person capacity spot is the Valley's authentic rock n' roll venue with fantastic sound and a grass-roots atmosphere. The restaurant serves typical bar food but is best known for its music.

Tip #83 Rockin' Kids Burbank

The award-winning Rockin' Kids Burbank lets parents chill while their kids play. This family-friendly spot is primarily for children aged seven and younger. Rated as one of the best places in LA for a party, it is the perfect place for birthdays, graduations, baptisms, baby showers, school trips, and family reunions.

Tip #84 iFLY Indoor Skydiving

Experience the sensation of flying in iFLY Indoor Skydiving's state-of-the-art vertical wind tunnels located on the Universal City Walk. Safe for all ages and abilities, indoor sky diving is an activity perfect for birthday parties, corporate events, team building, and more. Certified, world-class instructors coach classes for kids and adults and supervise parties while keeping things safe and fun.

iFLY uses science, technology, engineering, and math to design and operate vertical wind tunnels. This one-of-a-kind indoor skydiving experience is the thrill of a lifetime.

Chapter Review

- You can actually fly at Universal Studios City Walk thanks to iFly indoor skydiving.
- The Canyon in Woodland Hills is a great place to listen to live music.
- Burn off some energy at the Sky Zone Trampoline Park.
- Try an electric cart at K1 Speed Indoor Go-Karts.
- Throw a birthday party to remember at Rockin' Kids Burbank.

Chapter 9: Educational and Spiritual Places

The San Fernando Valley is home to many local colleges and spiritual spaces.

Tip #85 California State University Northridge

California State University, Northridge (CSUN or Cal State Northridge) is a public university with a total enrollment of nearly 40,000 students. It has the second-largest undergraduate population and the third-largest student body in the 23-campus Cal State system. It is also one of the largest n comprehensive universities in the United States.

CSUN offers 134 bachelor's and master's degree programs in 70 different fields, plus four doctoral degrees and 24 teaching credentials. CSUN also has one of the best music schools and film schools in the world. Home to the National Center on Deafness, the university hosts the annual International Conference on Technology and Persons with Disabilities, more commonly known as the CSUN Conference.

Tip #86 Los Angeles Valley College

Los Angeles Valley College (LAVC) is a public community college and part of the Los Angeles Community College District, the largest community college district in the country and one of the largest in the world.

The college is adjacent to Grant High School in Valley Glen. Often called "Valley College" or simply "Valley," it opened in 1949, at which time the campus was on the site of Van Nuys High School. The college moved to its current location in 1951. The 105-acre campus currently offers more than 140 associate degree programs and certificate programs.

Notable alumni include actor Sean Astin, best known for his role in the Lord of the Rings; actor and environmentalist Ed Begley Jr.; actor Bryan Cranston, who played Hal on Malcolm in the Middle; Walter White on the award-winning series Breaking Bad; musician Micky Dolenz of The Monkees; actor Tom Selleck of Magnum PI fame; and many more.

Tip #87 Pierce College

Also part of the Los Angeles Community College District, Pierce College, located in Woodland Hills, serves 22,000 students each semester. It's hard to believe how much the campus has evolved, particularly since it began with only 70 students and 18 faculty members in 1947. Originally known as the Clarence W. Pierce School of Agriculture, the institution's initial focus was crop cultivation and animal husbandry. Nine years later, in 1956, the school was renamed Los Angeles Pierce Junior College, retaining the name of its founder, Dr. Pierce, as well as his commitment to agricultural and veterinary study.

Offering 92 academic disciplines, students can also pursue any of the 44 associate degrees or 78 Certificates of Achievement.

Tip #88 Glendale Community College

Glendale Junior College was founded in 1927 to serve the Glendale Union High School District. Classes were initially held in Glendale Union High School. Two years later, the junior college moved to the

Harvard School plant of the Glendale Union High School District, where it remained until 1937. When the present building was completed in 1944, the name of the school was changed to Glendale College. With an open admissions policy, the college now offers credit for life experiences.

One interesting tidbit: Glendale Community College inspired the NBC show Community, which premiered in the fall of 2009. The show's creator, Dan Harmon, a Glendale Community College alum, described the series as "flawed characters [coming into Greendale] and becoming unflawed by being in this place because it's been underestimated by the system around it."

Tip #89 Mission San Fernando Rey de Espana

Founded in 1797, the Mission San Fernando Rey de España is a major part of Valley history. So important, both the San Fernando Valley and the city of San Fernando are named after it. Today, the mission grounds of this Catholic establishment also function as a museum. Native American designs decorate the walls of Mission San Fernando Rey Church. The elaborate altar and pulpit, carved from walnut, dated to 1687, were brought over from Spain. The mission includes a simple adobe church, the Convento, padre's quarters, and a guest house organized around a quadrangle. The Convento's 19 spectacular arches border the length of the building. Two beautifully landscaped gardens contain a sculpture of the mission's founder, Father Fermin Francisco de Lasuén.

The first time I visited was to celebrate St. Francis of Assisi Day with a Blessing of the Animals ceremony. We brought the family dog, Siesta, an ugly mutt who looked more like a giant rat than a Chihuahua mix. She wowed the crowd and the Priest giving out the blessing that day by doing the doggie dance and twirling on her hind legs. I'll never forget all the animals that were there that day getting blessed.

Tip #90 Wat Thai Temple

Wat Thai is the largest Thai Buddhist Temple in Los Angeles. Situated in the Sun Valley, about 15 miles north of downtown, Wat Thai replicates traditional Buddhist temples in Thailand. In addition, Wat Thai of Los Angeles serves as a religious and cultural center for the Thai community in Southern California.

The history and establishment of the temple is a long and complicated one. It's history dates back to a visit by a Thai Buddhist monk in 1970. At that time, his dream of setting up a Thai Buddhist temple was met with great enthusiasm. The Thai American Buddhist Association was eventually organized, and a group of three Buddhist monks got to work.

The first step was purchasing a suburban house on Sepulveda Boulevard to be converted into a residence for monks. Two acres of land were purchased in 1972 with donations from a wealthy Bangkok businessman. Blueprints to build a traditional Thai monastery with living quarters, a temple, and sacred buildings materialized. Today, Wat Thai offers regular services and teachings along with twelve festivals and celebrations annually.

- **New Year Festival**

On January 1st, the temple holds a festival following a chanting ceremony on New Year's Eve.

- **Magha Puja Day**

Taking place on the full moon of the third lunar month, usually in mid-February, Magha Puja Day is in commemoration of the Great Assembly of Disciples.

- **Wan Waikhru**

This observance can take place on any Thursday in January. Students show reverence for their teachers.

- **Songkran**

This Water Festival occurs on the second weekend of April.

- **Visakha Puja Day**

The full moon day of the sixth lunar month usually falls in the middle or end of May. It commemorates the birth, enlightenment, and passing away of the Buddha.

- **Lorthien or Candle-Casting Ceremony**

The day before Buddhist Lent, this ceremony happens any day in July.

- **Asalha Puja Day**

Occurs on the full moon day of the eighth lunar month, usually in the middle or towards the end of July, in commemoration of the Buddha's First Sermon.

- **H.M. the Queen's Birthday**

August 12th marks the birthday of the current queen of Thailand, Queen Suthida.

- **Salakapat Ceremony**

Coming near the end of August, this ceremony offers special utensils to the monks.

- **Ok Phansa**

Marks the end of Vassa, the period of retreat during the rains, which takes place on the full moon day of the eleventh month, usually in the middle or end of October.

- **Tot Kathin**

The Post-Lenten Robe-Offering Ceremony takes place on any day one month following Ok Pansa to present robes to the monks who have completed the Vassa.

- **H.M. the 9th King's Birthday**

The December 5th birthday of his Majesty, the Late King Bhumibol Adulyadej. On this day, pay their respects and honor him.

Along with the large population of Thai people and Thai Americans, refugees from Cambodia, Vietnam, and Laos participate in the religious activities of Wat Thai.

Tip #91 Forest Lawn in Glendale

On a clear day, you can see forever at Forest Lawn Memorial Park, a privately owned cemetery in Glendale that has been a local landmark for more than 100 years. The original flagship location of Forest Lawn Memorial-Parks & Mortuaries now includes six additional cemeteries and four more mortuaries in Southern California.

esides the many options available to honor your loved ones, Forest awn has a museum at the property with exhibits and special vents. First opened in 1952, the Museum is adjacent to the Hall of rucifixion-Resurrection at Forest Lawn – Glendale. Founder Dr. [ubert Eaton hoped the park would be "a place where artists study nd sketch; schoolteachers bring happy children to see the things ley read of in books."

n oil painting titled Song of the Angels by French artist William-dolphe Bouguereau (1825-19205) is one of the most coveted bjects in the Museum's permanent collection. Legend has it that ouguereau searched for a model for the painting's figures and had is first wife, Nelly Monochablon, pose as angels, one by one, and nally, with a child in her arms. The painting depicts a mother and hild sleeping in a pastoral scene while a trio of angels hovers earby.

ip #92 Transcendental Meditation in the San Fernando 'alley

'he Transcendental Meditation Center in the Valley has helped ountless people learn the art of Transcendental Meditation (TM). cholarships have been awarded to more than one million at-risk tudents, military veterans, homeless people, and others through artnerships with other non-profit organizations and foundations.

'ranscendental Meditation was brought to the West in 1959 by Iaharishi Mahesh Yogi. The Transcendental Meditation technique ; not a religion or philosophy but a simple technique for inner eace and wellness. Extensive research shows TM reduces stress nd anxiety.

Anyone can come to a free introductory talk held via conference ca
or online. TM instruction requires personal, one-on-one sessions
with a certified teacher. Therefore, it will not be taught during this
group introduction. However, you'll have the opportunity to meet
local teachers and sign up.

Tip #93 Bella's Psychic Insight

Clairvoyant and spiritual healer Bella A. and her spiritual sisters a
intuitive healers and clairvoyants. For the last 17 years, Bella A. ha
offered services from her Canoga Park headquarters. Bella A. has
received excellent reviews from her customers. Her main services
are:

- **Palmistry**

Palm reading or hand prediction is a tool to uncover a person's
fortune and future by analyzing their hands. Also known as
Chiromancy, a palm reader can predict health, wealth, wisdom,
career, and marriage, among other things.

- **Tarot Cards**

A tarot card reading may help you understand your journey throug
the spiritual, emotional, and physical world. The key to getting the
most from tarot cards is understanding what each card means
individually and how they work together to provide greater insight

- **Psychic Readings**

Good psychics analyze the energy from the past, present, and
future. They may explain points of connection to give you peace an
confidence about how your path has been, is, and will be
progressing.

- **Spiritual Tibetan Singing Bowl Healing**

very person's physical being is as unique as their spirituality.
Vhen Bella A. meets clients, she receives the knowledge,
iformation, and tools from the Lead Source/SPIRIT, ultimately
learing accrued negative energies with whatever is holding a
erson back from what they want to achieve.

ip #94 The Imagine Center for Lightworkers

ed by Goddess Tauheedah and embodying a light portal of love
nd higher consciousness, she and the Imagine Center staff provide
uidance and knowledge for your journey into higher light.

his spiritual center, located in Tarzana, is open to individuals or
roups for readings and class instruction. The shop's offerings
ppeal to anyone looking to add an extra layer of metaphysical
nowledge to his or her life. Music, books, crystals, stones, and
ewelry are available for purchase.

ersonal energy work is also available for those seeking awareness
nd spiritual healing. Healers move energy across the body and
oul to release stress and anxiety and expand awareness and
penness to the power of self-love. You'll receive chakra clearing,
nasculine-feminine alignment, and planetary grounding for
tability. All practitioners are certified and serve creatively with love
s their compass.

Chapter Review

- Don't miss seeing Mission San Fernando Rey de España, one
  of California's twenty-one Spanish Missions.
- Did you know Forest Lawn Cemetery in Glendale has a
  museum? Well, it does, and you should see it!

- Let Bella read your palm at Bella's Psychic Insight.
- Visit the Valley's Transcendental Meditation Center for a FREE introductory workshop.
- Get some energy work done by Goddess Tauheedah at the Imagine Center for Lightworkers.

Chapter 10: Things to Do with Your Four-Legged Family Member

With its warm weather and open spaces, the Valley is truly a mecca for dog lovers. Many restaurant patios also welcome furry companions for breakfast, lunch, or dinner.

Tip #95 Dog-Friendly Breweries

There's nothing like a cold beer on hot days in the Valley. The only thing that makes it better is bringing your dog along.

- House of Brews
  This cozy, dog-friendly spot in San Fernando is a local hangout. There are 30 beers on tap, 25 bottled beers, a full bar, a great wine selection, and classic bar food. In addition, the patio has music, trivia, and televised sports events.

- Shadow Grove Brewing
  You will find this dog-friendly brewery and tasting room in the heart of downtown San Fernando. The design of the 2,600 square foot building immerses human and dog guests into a storyline that is open to interpretation. Discover the characters of this story through the beers. Learn more about the environment and action in the tasting room. Let your imagination run wild at Shadow Grove Brewing.

Tip #96 West Valley and East Valley Animal Shelters

LA Animal Services run both; these are clean shelters with dogs and other animals waiting to find their forever homes. I rescued my first dog as an adult, Blondie, at the East Valley Shelter, and it was one of the best things I have ever done in my life. The shelters also offer free spay and neutering to locals without the means to do so on their own, along with microchipping, licensing, and more. During the week, you need an appointment to visit, but both sites are open to the public on the weekends. Both locals also have a lost pet database so if your fur baby goes missing while you're on vacation, check with the nearest shelter. Do yourself a favor and make sure your pet is microchipped and wearing an id tag at all times when on vacation.

Tip #97 Special Stores for Doggie Delights

- **Three Dog Bakery Encino**

Three barks, I mean cheers, for Three Dog Bakery Encino. The world's first bakery for dogs naturally makes the world's best dog treats. You and your furry friend will enjoy everything about this place. Since 1989, its owners have been selling top-quality dog food, chews, packaged treats, and, of course, their famous hand-baked treats and cakes for your pup.

- **Red Barn Feed and Saddlery**

Animal lovers in the San Fernando Valley have been coming here for more than 50 years. Why? Because the knowledgeable staff is passionate about customer service and every pet's needs. For this family-run operation, it's not so much a job but a way of life. Red Barn Feed and Saddlery carries livestock, including chicken coops, bird supplies, horse supplies, etc. Be advised that one of its employees is a cat. Yes, a cat. And every spring, live baby chicks are for sale.

Tip #98 Sepulveda Basin Off Leash Dog Park

Does your dog needs exercise? If the answer is yes, then the Sepulveda Basin Off-Leash Dog Park in Van Nuys is worth checking out. The park is divided into three separate sections for large, small,

nd timid dogs. There is an obstacle course, water stations, and
erimeter fencing. Remember that the park is closed on Fridays
om 6-11 a.m. for maintenance. But other than that, you'll find
ogs and their owners playing here.

ne time when I was there with my dog Baldwin, we got punked!
es, it's true. Unbeknownst to me, a television crew was there
hooting a show starring comedian Chelsea Handler. She walked up
) me complaining about the people having a picnic at the dog park
nd suggested I tell them to leave. So I walked over to the picnic
roup with Chelsea in tow, and when one of the women pulled out a
uge butterfly net to catch my dog and me in, I ran off and knew
/hat had happened. I never did find out what the show was or see
1e segment, but it was funny. And the kind of thing that happens
ll the time in the Valley.

ip: always bring plenty of water for your dog when hiking in the
alley, especially during summer months. Plus, watch for
attlesnakes starting in the spring.

ip #99 Westridge-Canyonback Wilderness Park

like the trails of Westridge-Canyonback Wilderness Park in Encino
/ith your faithful companion. Phenomenal views of the ocean and
owntown make the trip worthwhile. Located deep in the eastern
anta Monica Mountains, the Westridge fire road provides access
or hikers, mountain bikers, and equestrians along the north-south
idgeline. The park is contiguous with the 20,000-acre urban
/ilderness park known as the "Big Wild." Accessible from the San
ernando Valley at San Vincente Mountain Park, this park gets four
aws up!

Tip #100 Dog-Friendly Restaurants

Good dogs are invited to join their guardians at these Valley hot spots.

- **Gasolina Café**

Gasolina Cafe has a dog friendly, covered patio. The dishes made b
Chef Sandra Corderoat at this Woodland Hills restaurant on
Ventura Boulevard reflect her Spanish heritage. Jamon-wrapped
dates, Spring green paella, croquetas, and pan con tomate are just
few of the menu selections. Wine is made naturally and in small
batches.

- **The Fat Dog**

It's no surprise that this North Hollywood dog-themed gastropub i
pooch-friendly, with an airy patio that many four-legged friends
love to frequent. The owners have their own pups, so it's an ideal
stop for those looking to dine out with their dogs.

- **The Front Yard**

The Front Yard in North Hollywood has been a neighborhood
favorite since 2015. Nestled in the heart of the Arts District under
towering sycamores, it's open for indoor and outdoor dining seven
days a week. Hang out by the outdoor fireplace with your favorite
cocktail and pooch by your side. The Front Yard has an impressive
craft beer list and a long bar food menu. Try the Swedish meatball:

- **Granville**

This dog-friendly collection of modern-casual restaurants
specializes in wholesome, hand-crafted recipes and libations. With

lobally inspired food and music, this place fosters a culture of love
nd integrity in life and business. These restaurants support local,
rganic, and certified humane practices and make food from
cratch daily. Lunch, dinner, weekend breakfast, and bar are
vailable in a casual yet tasteful environment.

- **Añejo Cantina & Grill**

'his dog lovers' place is the trendiest Mexican restaurant in
herman Oaks. It has a full menu of delectable dishes and mouth-
vatering flavors. Guests enjoy Mexico's vibrant foods and ambiance
vith traditional recipes, late night entertainment, and an
xceptional banquet. Bottomless mimosas come with brunch!

ip #101 Best Friends Animal Rescue

'his Mission Hills Lifesaving Center is a part of Best Friends
nimal Society. It's a place to adopt dogs and other pets, but it's
lso on a mission to stop the killing of dogs and cats in shelters
ationwide. Best Friends launched NKLA (No-Kill Los Angeles) in
012 and gave more than $1.4 million to NKLA coalition groups in
017 to save newborn kittens, senior dogs, cats, and pit bull terriers.
ome of those funds also helped spay and neuter over 6,000 cats
nd dogs in underserved areas. The Rescue has also transferred
nore than 24,000 dogs and cats from LA animal shelters to the
Jission Hills pet adoption center and performed more than 25,000
pay/neuter procedures for LAAS and public pets combined. Those
nimals also received rabies vaccines and microchips. Since 2012,
est Friends has invested, on average, over $3.5 million annually to
perate the Northeast Valley Shelter.

During a recent Best Friends Super Adoption, local shelters and
escue groups brought animals to one central location to help them

find homes. More than 10,000 people attended, and 650 pets were adopted.

The Mission Hills location also participates in the annual Best Friends Strut Your Mutt event. Held in cities nationwide, Strut Your Mutt is a fundraiser and dog walk. Last year, approximately 5,000 people attended the LA Strut Your Mutt and raised more than $600,000 for 21 rescue groups.

Chapter Review

Visit the outside patio of a dog-friendly brewery like House of Brews and enjoy a brewski together. Don't feed your dog beer!

Hike the trails at Westridge-Canyonback Wilderness Park in Encino, and stop for the breathtaking views, and give your dog a break. Tip: always bring plenty of water for your dog, especially when hiking in the hot San Fernando Valley summer.

Enjoy dinner together at a local fav, The Front Yard in North Hollywood.

If your dog gets lost while in the Valley, there are two shelters to check with. Make sure your dog has a collar with your phone number and is microchipped before taking a vacation together anywhere.

Head to the Sepulveda Basin Off-Leash Dog Park, where both of you can meet new friends, both two-legged and four.

Save a life and adopt a dog from Best Friends Animal Shelter.

There's so much more to say about the San Fernando Valley. As mentioned above, I grew up there in a sun-kissed neighborhood surrounded by rolling, green hills with soaring mountains as a backdrop. We were the first family to own the ranch-style home in Northridge with a huge backyard. Life seemed simpler back then— but you can still find simple pleasures by visiting and learning about the San Fernando Valley.

I had the opportunity to move back to my family home after my mother died to help care for my ailing father. He had Parkinson's Disease. It was a very challenging time for me overseeing his care but being back in the Valley gave me the comfort I needed. The Valley has always been a special place for me. Writing these 101 Tips brought back many happy memories and made me fall in love with it all over again. I guess I'll always be a Valley girl at heart.

About the Author

Susan Hartzler is an award-winning writer and author of the memoir I'm Not Single, I Have a Dog: Dating Tales from the Bark Side, published by McFarland Publishers. It's available on Amazon and includes personal stories and pictures of her family home, a ranch-style beauty in Northridge. She is also a lifelong dog lover whose current pack of two beautiful Australian Shepherds, both professional actors and models, is represented by the prestigious animal talent agency LePaws. Together, they work as a Therapy Dog team visiting kids at local high schools and others who are in the hospital needing a little bit of doggie love.

HowExpert publishes how to guides by everyday experts. Visit HowExpert.com to learn more.

Recommended Resources

HowExpert.com – Quick 'How To' Guides on All Topics from A to Z by Everyday Experts.
HowExpert.com/free – Free HowExpert Email Newsletter.
HowExpert.com/books – HowExpert Books
HowExpert.com/courses – HowExpert Courses
HowExpert.com/clothing – HowExpert Clothing
HowExpert.com/membership – HowExpert Membership Site
HowExpert.com/affiliates – HowExpert Affiliate Program
HowExpert.com/jobs – HowExpert Jobs
HowExpert.com/writers – Write About Your #1 Passion/Knowledge/Expertise & Become a HowExpert Author.
HowExpert.com/resources – Additional HowExpert Recommended Resources
YouTube.com/HowExpert – Subscribe to HowExpert YouTube.
Instagram.com/HowExpert – Follow HowExpert on Instagram.
Facebook.com/HowExpert – Follow HowExpert on Facebook.
TikTok.com/@HowExpert – Follow HowExpert on TikTok.

Made in United States
North Haven, CT
13 August 2022